Canon EOS R50 Handbook for Beginners

Achieving Stunning Results in Photography

Rute Terra

Copyright © 2024 **Rute Terra**

This book or parts thereof may not be reproduced in any form, stored in any retrieval system, or transmitted in any form by any means—electronic, mechanical, photocopy, recording, or otherwise—without prior written permission of the publisher, except as provided by United States of America copyright law and fair use.

Disclaimer and Terms of Use

The author and publisher of this book and the accompanying materials have used their best efforts in preparing this book. The author and publisher make no representation or warranties with respect to the accuracy, applicability, fitness, or completeness of the contents of this book. The information contained in this book is strictly for informational purposes. Therefore, if you wish to apply the ideas contained in this book, you are taking full responsibility for your actions.

Printed in the United States of America

TABLE OF CONTENTS

TABLE OF CONTENTS III

CHAPTER 1 1

INTRODUCTION TO THE CANON EOS R50 1
- Overview of the Camera and Its Key Features 1
- Mirrorless Technology and the EOS R System 5
- Who Should Use the Canon EOS R50? (Beginners vs. Professionals) 9

CHAPTER 2 16

SETTING UP YOUR CANON EOS R50 16
- Unboxing and Assembling the Camera 16
- Basic Settings and Customization 26
- Firmware Updates and Camera Maintenance 30

CHAPTER 3 36

NAVIGATING THE CAMERA'S INTERFACE 36
- Buttons, Dials, and Touchscreen Controls 36
- Menu System Overview 43
- Customizing Function Buttons and Shortcuts 47

CHAPTER 4 52

UNDERSTANDING EXPOSURE AND FOCUS 52
- Exposure Basics: Aperture, Shutter Speed, ISO 52
- Autofocus Modes and Area Selection 58
- Metering Modes and Exposure Compensation 66

CHAPTER 5 72

CREATIVE SHOOTING MODES 72
- Manual, Aperture Priority, Shutter Priority, and Program Modes 72
- Scene Modes and Creative Filters 79
- Using the HDR and Panorama Features 86

CHAPTER 6 91

ADVANCED PHOTOGRAPHY TECHNIQUES 91
- Long Exposure and Night Photography 91
- Using Focus Bracketing and Stacking 95
- High-Speed Burst and Action Shots 102

CHAPTER 7 108

WORKING WITH LENSES AND ACCESSORIES 108

LENS COMPATIBILITY AND MOUNT ADAPTER OPTIONS 108
USING LENS FILTERS AND OTHER ACCESSORIES 112
WORKING WITH EXTERNAL FLASHES AND TRIPODS 117

CHAPTER 8 121

VIDEO RECORDING WITH THE CANON EOS R50 121

VIDEO SETTINGS AND FRAME RATES 121
AUDIO RECORDING: INTERNAL AND EXTERNAL MICROPHONES 123
BASIC TIPS FOR VIDEO EDITING 128

CHAPTER 9 131

CONNECTIVITY AND IMAGE SHARING 131

CONNECTING TO WI-FI AND BLUETOOTH ON THE CANON EOS R50 131
REMOTE SHOOTING WITH THE CANON APP 134
TRANSFERRING IMAGES TO MOBILE DEVICES OR COMPUTERS 139

CHAPTER 10 143

TROUBLESHOOTING AND MAINTENANCE 143

COMMON CAMERA ISSUES AND SOLUTIONS 143
CLEANING AND CARING FOR THE CAMERA 147
TIPS FOR LONG-TERM MAINTENANCE AND FIRMWARE UPGRADES 152

GLOSSARY 158

CHAPTER 1

INTRODUCTION TO THE CANON EOS R50

Overview of the Camera and Its Key Features

The **Canon EOS R50** is a powerful and versatile mirrorless camera designed to cater to both beginners and professionals alike. It is part of Canon's EOS R series, which combines high-quality imaging performance with advanced technology, all within a compact and lightweight body. In this section, we will explore the camera's essential features in detail, breaking down the technical terms and explaining how these features enhance the overall photography and videography experience.

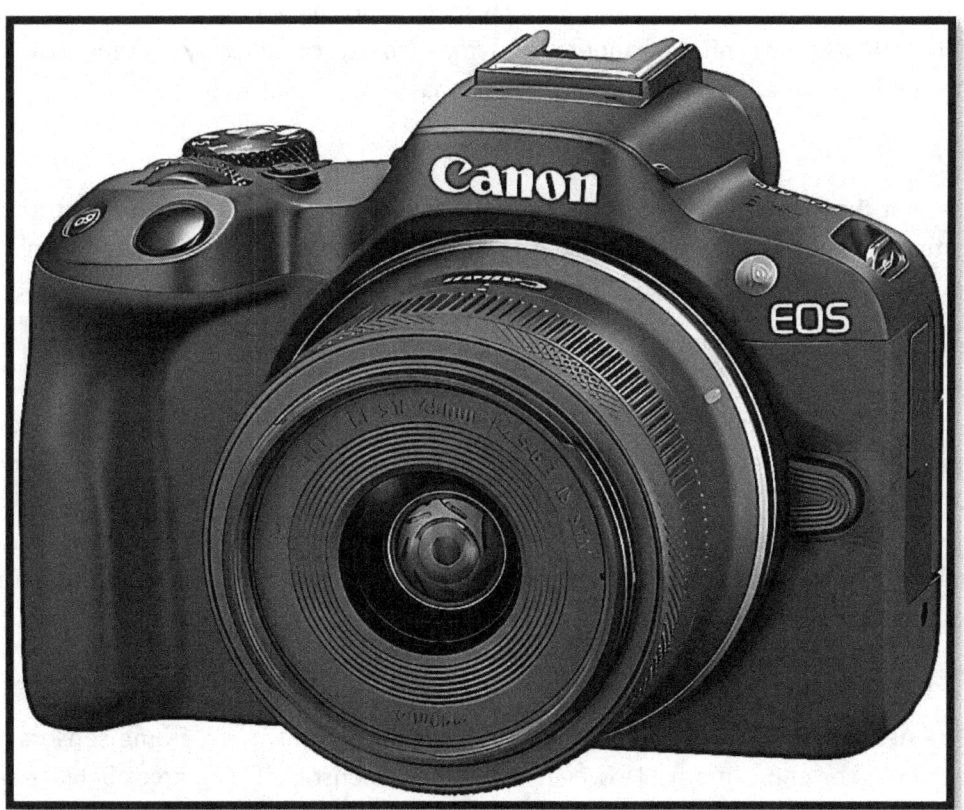

1. Mirrorless Design and Compact Form Factor

One of the most important aspects of the Canon EOS R50 is its **mirrorless design**, which makes the camera more compact and lightweight compared to traditional DSLR cameras. To understand why this is significant, let's break down the difference between **mirrorless cameras** and **DSLRs**.

- **Mirrorless vs. DSLR**:

    Traditional DSLR cameras use a mirror inside the camera body to reflect light from the lens up into an optical viewfinder. This mirror mechanism adds bulk to the camera, making DSLRs heavier and larger. In a mirrorless camera like the EOS R50, there is no mirror, allowing light to pass directly from the lens to the image sensor. This streamlined design eliminates the need for a bulky mirror and optical viewfinder, resulting in a smaller, lighter camera without sacrificing image quality.

- **Compact and Portable**:

    The compact size of the EOS R50 makes it highly portable and easy to carry around, whether you are traveling, shooting events, or using it for everyday photography. It's designed to fit comfortably in your hand and is small enough to fit into a backpack or camera bag without taking up too much space. This makes the EOS R50 an ideal choice for both beginner photographers who may not want to carry a heavy camera and professionals who need a lightweight secondary camera for specific shoots.

2. 24.2-Megapixel APS-C Sensor

At the heart of the Canon EOS R50 is its **24.2-megapixel APS-C CMOS sensor**. The sensor is a critical component of any camera because it's responsible for capturing light and turning it into an image. Let's break down what these technical terms mean and how they affect your photography.

- **Megapixels**:
    The number of megapixels refers to the resolution of the camera's sensor, or how much detail the camera can capture. The EOS R50's 24.2-megapixel sensor is capable of producing sharp, detailed images that can be printed in large sizes or cropped without losing significant quality. Whether you're shooting portraits, landscapes, or action shots, the high resolution gives you the flexibility to edit and enhance your photos in post-production.

- **APS-C Sensor**:

    The APS-C sensor in the EOS R50 is slightly smaller than the full-frame sensors found in some higher-end cameras. However, this type of sensor offers a great balance between image quality and cost. APS-C sensors provide a **crop factor** of 1.6x, meaning they effectively extend the reach of your lenses, making them ideal for wildlife or sports photography where zooming in is essential. The sensor is large enough to capture excellent detail and color, while also providing good performance in low-light situations.

3. Dual Pixel CMOS Autofocus II System

The Canon EOS R50 is equipped with the advanced **Dual Pixel CMOS Autofocus II** system, which allows for fast, accurate, and reliable autofocus performance. This feature is particularly important for both beginners and professionals, as it ensures that your subjects remain in sharp focus, even in challenging shooting conditions.

- **Fast and Accurate Autofocus**:

The Dual Pixel CMOS AF II system uses phase-detection pixels across the sensor to lock onto subjects quickly and accurately. This is crucial for capturing fast-moving subjects like pets, athletes, or children, as well as for ensuring that stationary subjects are in sharp focus, even when shooting in low light or with a shallow depth of field.

- **Eye and Face Detection**:

One of the standout features of the autofocus system is its **eye and face detection** capabilities. This means the camera can automatically detect and track human faces and eyes, keeping them in focus throughout the shot. For portrait photographers, this is invaluable, as it ensures that the most important part of the image—your subject's eyes—are always sharp and clear.

- **Animal and Vehicle Detection**:

In addition to human subjects, the EOS R50 can also detect animals and vehicles, making it a versatile tool for wildlife photography, pet portraits, and even automotive photography. Whether you're photographing a moving car or a running dog, the camera's intelligent autofocus system helps you keep the subject in focus.

4. 4K Video Recording

In addition to still photography, the Canon EOS R50 excels at **video recording**, offering **4K video resolution** at up to 30 frames per second (fps). This makes it a great option for videographers, vloggers, and content creators looking for high-quality video capture in a compact form.

- **4K Resolution:**

4K video recording provides four times the resolution of Full HD, resulting in ultra-sharp, detailed footage that looks professional even on large screens. Whether you're recording a family vacation, a YouTube vlog, or a professional video project, the EOS R50 delivers crisp, high-quality video that's perfect for modern viewing platforms.

- **Smooth Frame Rates:**

The camera can record in **4K at 30 fps**, which is ideal for most video content. If you need even smoother motion, you can switch to **Full HD at 60 fps**, which is great for recording fast-moving subjects or creating slow-motion effects in post-production.

- **Advanced Video Features**:

    The EOS R50 also includes **Canon's Movie Digital IS**, a digital image stabilization system that helps reduce camera shake while recording handheld. This is particularly useful for vloggers or filmmakers who may not always have access to a tripod or gimbal.

5. Vari-Angle Touchscreen LCD

The Canon EOS R50 is equipped with a **3-inch vari-angle touchscreen LCD**, which provides a flexible and user-friendly interface for both shooting and reviewing images.

- **Fully Articulating Screen**:

    The vari-angle screen can be tilted and rotated to accommodate a variety of shooting angles, making it easier to shoot from high, low, or awkward positions. This is especially useful for vloggers who need to film themselves or for photographers trying to capture creative perspectives.

- **Touchscreen Controls**:

    The touchscreen interface allows you to navigate the camera's menus, adjust settings, and even focus on your subject by simply tapping the screen. This intuitive control system makes the camera accessible to beginners who may not be familiar with all the buttons and dials, while also speeding up workflow for professionals who need quick access to settings.

6. Wi-Fi and Bluetooth Connectivity

In the age of social media and instant sharing, the Canon EOS R50 offers built-in **Wi-Fi and Bluetooth** connectivity, allowing you to easily transfer images and videos to your smartphone, tablet, or computer.

- **Wireless Image Transfer**:

    With the Canon Camera Connect app, you can wirelessly transfer photos and videos directly from your camera to your mobile device. This is perfect for photographers on the go who need to share images quickly without the hassle of cables or external memory card readers.

- **Remote Shooting**:

    The app also allows for **remote shooting**, meaning you can control your camera from your smartphone. This is useful for self-portraits, group shots, or situations where you need to set up the camera in a hard-to-reach location and trigger the shutter remotely.

Conclusion

The Canon EOS R50 is packed with features that cater to both beginners and professionals, making it an incredibly versatile camera. Its **compact mirrorless design, high-resolution sensor, advanced autofocus system, 4K video capabilities, vari-angle touchscreen,** and **wireless connectivity** all contribute to its status as a powerful tool for a wide range of photography and videography needs. Whether you're just starting your photography journey or looking for a compact, high-performance camera to complement your professional gear, the EOS R50 offers a fantastic balance of portability, functionality, and image quality.

Mirrorless Technology and the EOS R System

The Canon EOS R50 belongs to Canon's **EOS R series**, a lineup of mirrorless cameras designed to offer high-quality imaging and advanced features in a more compact and efficient form compared to traditional DSLR cameras. In this section, we'll dive deep into what **mirrorless technology** is, how it differs from DSLRs, and why the EOS R system stands out as a revolutionary development in photography. This explanation will break down the technical terms into simple, easy-to-understand concepts for both beginners and professionals.

1. What is Mirrorless Technology?

At the core of the Canon EOS R50's design is its **mirrorless technology**. To fully appreciate this feature, it's important to understand what a mirrorless camera is and how it differs from a DSLR.

- **How a DSLR Works**:

  In a traditional DSLR (Digital Single-Lens Reflex) camera, there's a mirror inside the camera body that reflects light from the lens up into an optical viewfinder. When you take a picture, the mirror flips up, allowing light to hit the image sensor and capture the photo. This mechanical process adds bulk to the camera and involves moving parts, which can sometimes cause noise and slight delays.

- **How a Mirrorless Camera Works**:

  In contrast, a **mirrorless camera** like the Canon EOS R50 does not have a mirror. Instead, light passes directly from the lens to the image sensor, which captures the image and displays a live view on an electronic viewfinder (EVF) or the rear screen. This direct process eliminates the need for the mirror mechanism, allowing for a more compact and lightweight camera body.

Key Advantages of Mirrorless Technology:

- **Compact and Lightweight Design**:

  One of the most immediate benefits of mirrorless technology is the **reduced size and weight** of the camera. Without the mirror and optical viewfinder, mirrorless cameras like the Canon EOS R50 are smaller and easier to carry around, making them ideal for travel, street photography, or even professional shoots where portability is key. This design allows photographers to be more mobile and less burdened by heavy gear.

- **Faster, Quieter Operation**:

The lack of a mirror means that there are fewer moving parts inside a mirrorless camera, which translates into faster and quieter operation. When you take a picture with a mirrorless camera, you don't hear the loud "click" associated with the mirror flipping up in a DSLR. This can be an advantage in situations where silence is important, such as during weddings, wildlife photography, or events where you don't want to disturb your subjects.

- **Real-Time Preview with the Electronic Viewfinder (EVF)**:

Mirrorless cameras like the EOS R50 use an **electronic viewfinder (EVF)** or a rear LCD screen to display what the camera's sensor is capturing in real time. This live view shows exactly how the final image will look, including exposure, white balance, and depth of field. With a DSLR, you only get this preview after taking the photo and reviewing it on the back screen. With mirrorless, what you see is what you get, helping both beginners and professionals fine-tune their settings before taking the shot.

- **Improved Autofocus Performance**:

Mirrorless cameras, particularly those in Canon's EOS R series, benefit from **on-sensor phase detection autofocus**. In a DSLR, autofocus relies on a separate sensor system, which can sometimes result in slower or less accurate focusing, especially when shooting video or using live view. Mirrorless cameras, on the other hand, use the main image sensor to handle autofocus, offering faster and more precise results. This is especially important for action photography, sports, or any situation where speed is critical.

2. Canon EOS R System: A New Era in Photography

The Canon EOS R50 is part of Canon's **EOS R system**, a groundbreaking series of mirrorless cameras and lenses that redefine image quality, speed, and functionality. Let's explore the key elements of the EOS R system that make it stand out.

Key Features of the EOS R System:

- **The RF Mount**:

At the heart of the EOS R system is the **RF lens mount**, which represents a major leap forward in lens and camera design. The RF mount has a **54mm diameter** and a **short 20mm flange distance** (the distance between the lens mount and the sensor). This design allows for larger lenses with wider apertures and more flexibility in optical design. For professionals, this means access to some of the sharpest, fastest lenses ever made by Canon. For beginners, it means exceptional image quality right out of the box, even with standard kit lenses.

Why the RF Mount Matters:

The larger mount allows more light to reach the sensor, improving image quality, especially in low-light situations. It also allows Canon to design lenses with improved sharpness, faster autofocus, and better image stabilization. Whether you're shooting portraits, landscapes, or action, the RF mount's advantages result in sharper images with more accurate focus and reduced aberrations.

- **Advanced Image Processing with the DIGIC X Processor**:

The EOS R50, like other cameras in the EOS R series, uses Canon's latest **DIGIC X image processor**. This powerful processor enhances the camera's speed, image quality, and overall performance.

  - **Faster Performance**:

  The DIGIC X processor enables faster continuous shooting speeds, allowing the EOS R50 to capture up to **12 frames per second** in electronic shutter mode. This is especially useful for sports or wildlife photographers who need to capture fast-moving subjects.

  - **Better Image Quality**:

  The processor also plays a key role in improving image quality. It helps reduce noise in low-light situations, allowing photographers to shoot at higher ISO levels without compromising image clarity. This means that even in challenging lighting conditions, the EOS R50 can produce sharp, well-exposed images.

- **Dual Pixel CMOS Autofocus II**:

A hallmark of the EOS R system is its **Dual Pixel CMOS Autofocus (AF) II** technology, which provides fast, smooth, and accurate autofocus for both stills and video. Unlike older autofocus systems that use a separate phase detection module, Dual Pixel AF uses the entire sensor to perform phase detection, making autofocus faster and more reliable.

  - **Eye and Face Detection**:

  One of the most notable features of Dual Pixel CMOS AF II is **eye and face detection**, which automatically tracks and focuses on a subject's eyes, ensuring that portraits and close-ups are always sharp. This feature is especially beneficial for beginners, who may not yet be comfortable manually focusing on their subject's eyes, and for professionals who need precise autofocus for critical shots.

- **Animal and Vehicle Detection**:

    The EOS R system takes autofocus to the next level by offering **animal and vehicle detection**. Whether you're photographing pets, wildlife, or fast-moving cars, the camera's autofocus system is intelligent enough to recognize and track these subjects, keeping them in sharp focus throughout the shot.

3. Why Mirrorless Technology and the EOS R System Matter for Photographers

Now that we've covered the technical aspects of mirrorless technology and the EOS R system, let's discuss why these innovations are so important for both beginners and professionals.

For Beginners:

- **Ease of Use**:

    Mirrorless cameras like the EOS R50 are generally easier to use than DSLRs, especially for those who are just starting out in photography. The **real-time EVF** and touchscreen display make it easy to see exactly what your final image will look like before you even press the shutter. This helps new photographers learn how different settings (like exposure and white balance) affect their photos in real time.

- **Portability**:

    Beginners often prioritize portability, especially if they're using their camera for travel, social events, or casual everyday photography. The compact size of the EOS R50 makes it easy to carry around, meaning beginners are more likely to take it with them and get more practice.

- **Automatic Modes and Assistance**:

    The EOS R50 includes a variety of automatic modes and scene presets that make it easier for beginners to take great photos without fully understanding all the technical settings. The camera's intelligent autofocus, face detection, and exposure control allow beginners to focus on composition and creativity while the camera handles the technical details.

For Professionals:

1. **Superior Image Quality and Performance**:

    The combination of the **RF mount**, **DIGIC X processor**, and **Dual Pixel AF II** means the EOS R50 delivers outstanding image quality and performance. Professionals who need high-resolution images, fast autofocus, and reliable performance in a variety of shooting conditions will appreciate the capabilities of this camera.

2. **Advanced Features for Creative Control**:

   While the EOS R50 is beginner-friendly, it also offers full manual control, allowing professionals to fine-tune every aspect of their photography. The **customizable buttons**, **high-speed continuous shooting**, and advanced autofocus modes provide the flexibility that professionals need to capture complex or fast-paced scenes.

3. **Versatile Lens Options**:

   The **RF lens system** offers professionals access to a wide range of high-performance lenses, from wide-angle primes to telephoto zooms. For professionals who require specialized lenses for different types of photography (like portrait, macro, or sports), the EOS R system offers the flexibility to switch between high-quality lenses without compromising performance.

Conclusion

Mirrorless technology and the Canon EOS R system represent a significant leap forward in photography, offering both beginners and professionals a range of powerful features that enhance image quality, speed, and ease of use. Whether you're just starting your photography journey or are a seasoned professional, the Canon EOS R50 provides a compact, reliable, and highly capable tool that leverages the best of mirrorless innovation. By understanding how mirrorless technology works and why the EOS R system is designed the way it is, you can unlock the full potential of this impressive camera, improving your skills and achieving outstanding results in your photography.

Who Should Use the Canon EOS R50? (Beginners vs. Professionals)

The Canon EOS R50 is a mirrorless camera designed to meet the needs of a wide range of photographers, from those just starting their journey to seasoned professionals. It combines user-friendly features with advanced capabilities, making it a versatile tool for various shooting styles and skill levels. In this section, we'll explore who should use the Canon EOS R50, breaking down its appeal to both **beginners** and **professionals** and how each group can make the most of this camera.

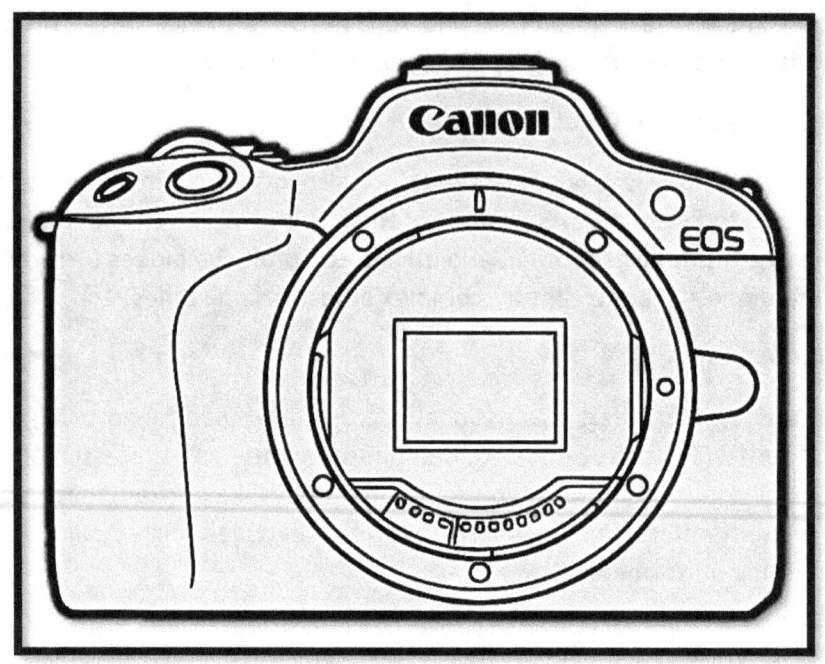

1. Why the Canon EOS R50 is Perfect for Beginners

For those new to photography, the Canon EOS R50 offers an ideal balance between ease of use and high-quality results. It is packed with features that make learning photography enjoyable, while also providing room for growth as users develop their skills. Here's why the EOS R50 is a great choice for beginners:

Ease of Use with Intuitive Features

The Canon EOS R50 is designed to be beginner-friendly, with a range of features that simplify the photography process:

- **Auto Modes and Scene Presets**:

    Beginners may feel overwhelmed by the technical aspects of photography, such as adjusting exposure, shutter speed, or aperture. The EOS R50 comes equipped with automatic shooting modes and scene presets, which allow new users to focus on composition and creativity while the camera handles the technical settings. For instance, the camera's **Scene Intelligent Auto mode** analyzes the scene and selects the appropriate settings for the best possible image, making it easy to capture great shots without needing to understand complex manual controls.

- **Guided User Interface**:

Canon has designed the EOS R50 with a **guided interface** that explains different shooting modes and settings in simple terms. This is particularly useful for beginners who may not be familiar with photography jargon. The interface helps new users understand the impact of different settings on their photos, acting as a built-in tutorial that enhances learning while shooting.

- **Touchscreen Controls**:

    The camera's **vari-angle touchscreen** is easy to navigate, allowing users to quickly adjust settings, focus, and review images with a simple tap or swipe. This intuitive control system feels familiar to anyone used to smartphones, making the transition to a more advanced camera smooth for beginners.

Compact and Lightweight Design

One of the main barriers for beginners is the size and weight of traditional cameras, which can feel cumbersome and intimidating. The Canon EOS R50 solves this problem with its **compact and lightweight body**, making it easy to carry around and use in various environments.

- **Portability**:
    The camera's small size and light weight make it ideal for beginners who want a camera they can take anywhere, whether for travel photography, casual everyday shooting, or documenting special events. The compact design encourages new photographers to experiment with their camera more frequently, leading to faster learning and improvement.

- **Easy to Handle**:

    Beginners often struggle with the ergonomics of larger, more complex cameras. The EOS R50 is designed with a comfortable grip and simple button layout, making it easy to handle and control. This ensures that new users can focus on capturing their shots rather than fumbling with difficult controls.

Learning and Growing with the Camera

The Canon EOS R50 is not just for taking beginner-level snapshots; it offers plenty of room for growth as users become more confident in their photography skills:

- **Manual Controls for Advanced Learning**:

    As beginners gain more experience, they will likely want to take more control over their photography settings. The EOS R50 provides full **manual mode** options, allowing users to experiment with exposure, aperture, and shutter speed as they become more comfortable with the camera. This gradual progression from automatic to manual control makes the EOS R50 a camera that can grow with the user's skill level.

- **Learning Photography with Canon's Creative Assist**:

    The EOS R50 also features **Creative Assist**, a mode that simplifies complex settings by presenting them in more understandable terms, such as adjusting brightness, background blur, and color tone. For a beginner who is eager to learn, this feature acts as a bridge between auto modes and full manual control, allowing them to experiment with different creative effects without being overwhelmed by technical terms.

- **Access to Educational Resources**:

    Canon offers a wealth of resources, including tutorials, tips, and online communities, to help beginners make the most of their EOS R50. From video tutorials on YouTube to detailed guides available on Canon's website, new photographers have plenty of support to help them master the camera and improve their skills.

2. Why Professionals Should Consider the Canon EOS R50

While the Canon EOS R50 is highly accessible to beginners, it also packs enough advanced features to make it a worthy addition to a professional's toolkit. Here's why professionals may find the EOS R50 valuable:

High-Quality Imaging in a Compact Package

Professionals often need high-performance gear that delivers excellent results without weighing them down. The Canon EOS R50 strikes this balance, offering professional-level image quality in a small and convenient body.

- **Impressive Image Quality**:

    Despite its compact size, the EOS R50 is equipped with a **24.2-megapixel APS-C CMOS sensor**, delivering sharp, detailed images that meet the standards of professional photography. Whether shooting portraits, landscapes, or product photos, the EOS R50 provides rich, vibrant colors and high dynamic range, ensuring that professional photographers can achieve stunning results.

- **Advanced Autofocus for Precision Shooting**:

    The EOS R50 features **Dual Pixel CMOS Autofocus II**, which offers fast and accurate autofocus performance, even in challenging conditions. This is a key feature for professionals who need to capture fast-moving subjects, such as during sports events, wildlife photography, or dynamic street scenes. The camera's ability to track eyes, faces, and even animals makes it a reliable tool for professionals who require precision and speed in their work.

Portability for On-the-Go Professionals

Many professionals need a secondary camera that is easy to carry but doesn't compromise on quality. The Canon EOS R50's lightweight and compact design make it a great choice for photographers who need a more portable option without sacrificing performance.

- **Travel and Street Photography**:

   For professional photographers who travel frequently or shoot in urban environments, the EOS R50's compact size allows for discreet and convenient shooting. It's less conspicuous than a larger DSLR, making it easier to blend in with the surroundings and capture candid moments without drawing attention.

- **Backup Camera for Professionals**:

   Many professionals use the EOS R50 as a **backup camera**. It's perfect for those moments when a lighter, more compact camera is needed, or for situations where carrying a full-sized DSLR would be impractical. Despite its size, the EOS R50 can still deliver the image quality required for professional work, making it a reliable companion on any shoot.

Video Capabilities for Professional Content Creators

In today's digital world, many professionals, including photographers, are expanding their work into video content. The Canon EOS R50 offers powerful video features that make it suitable for professional content creation:

- **4K Video Recording**:

   The EOS R50 is capable of recording **4K video** at 30 frames per second, making it an excellent tool for professional videographers or photographers who want to add video to their portfolio. Whether capturing cinematic footage, shooting interviews, or creating content for social media, the EOS R50's video quality meets professional standards.

- **Advanced Audio Controls**:

   For professionals who are serious about video production, the EOS R50 provides external microphone input, allowing for high-quality audio capture. This is especially important for vlogging, YouTube content creation, or interviews where clear, professional-level audio is essential.

- **Ease of Use for Vlogging and Social Media**:

The camera's **vari-angle touchscreen** and lightweight design make it perfect for vlogging or creating social media content. Professionals who need to create high-quality videos on the go can rely on the EOS R50's user-friendly interface and video capabilities to produce polished content quickly and efficiently.

3. Canon EOS R50 for Both Beginners and Professionals: A Versatile Camera

The Canon EOS R50 is designed to cater to a wide audience, offering features that are beneficial to both beginners and professionals. Its versatility makes it a unique camera that bridges the gap between entry-level users and experienced photographers. Here's why the EOS R50 appeals to both groups:

Shared Features for Beginners and Professionals

While beginners and professionals may use the EOS R50 differently, there are several features that appeal to both:

- **High Image Quality**:

    Both beginners and professionals want to capture high-quality images, and the EOS R50 delivers in this area with its powerful sensor and image processor. Beginners will appreciate the ease with which they can achieve beautiful photos, while professionals will be impressed by the level of detail and sharpness the camera provides.

- **Creative Flexibility**:

    The EOS R50 allows for creative expression at any skill level. Beginners can explore different **scene modes** and presets, while professionals can take full control over settings with **manual mode**. Both groups can experiment with the camera's **Creative Assist** feature to fine-tune their images and try out different artistic effects.

- **Portability and Convenience**:

    Whether you're a beginner taking your camera out for a casual day of shooting or a professional using it as a backup on a major project, the compact design of the EOS R50 makes it a convenient option for all photographers. Its small size and lightweight body ensure that it's always easy to carry, without compromising on quality or performance.

Conclusion

The Canon EOS R50 is a versatile and powerful camera that caters to both beginners and professionals. Its user-friendly features make it accessible to new photographers, helping them learn and grow with the camera, while its advanced capabilities ensure that professionals can rely on it for high-quality results in a variety of situations. Whether you're just starting out or are an experienced photographer, the EOS R50 provides the tools and flexibility needed to capture stunning images and videos, making it a camera that grows with your skills and continues to meet your creative needs.

CHAPTER 2

SETTING UP YOUR CANON EOS R50

Unboxing and Assembling the Camera

When purchasing a new camera, especially a versatile tool like the Canon EOS R50, unboxing and assembling can feel like an exciting step. It's the moment you get hands-on with the equipment, and for both beginners and professionals, starting on the right foot is crucial. In this section, we'll walk through the unboxing experience, explain each component you'll encounter, and guide you step-by-step on assembling the camera.

1. Unboxing the Canon EOS R50

The unboxing process is often the first tactile experience you'll have with your new camera, so it's important to understand what each item in the box is and how to handle it.

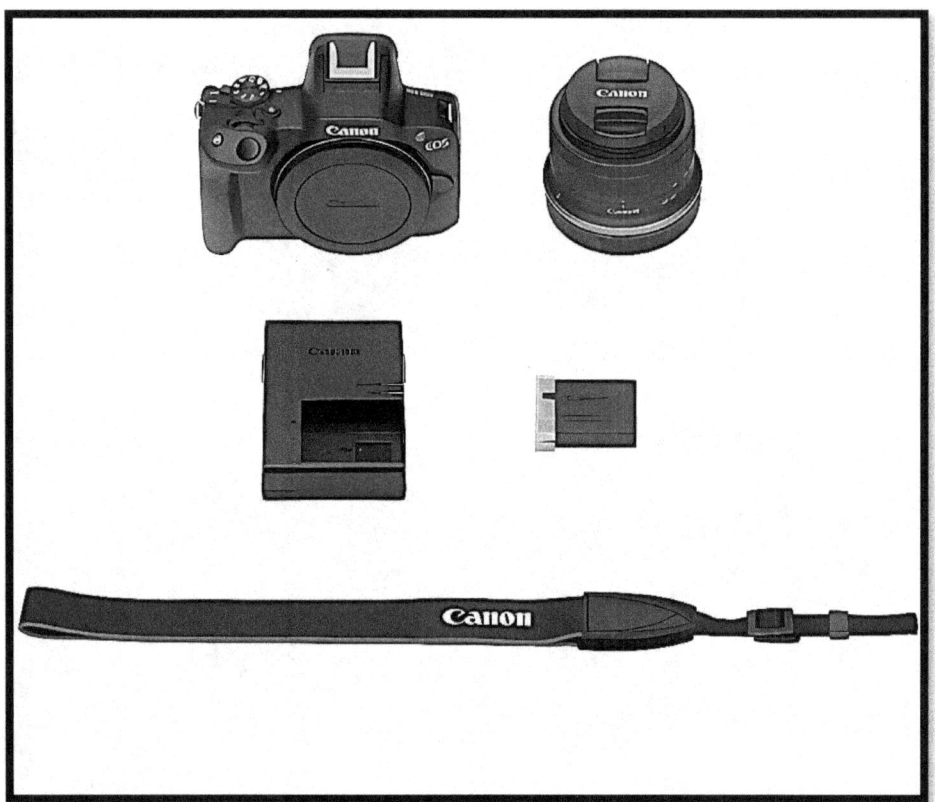

What to Expect Inside the Box:

When you open the Canon EOS R50 box, you'll find several items neatly packed and organized. These typically include:

- **The Camera Body**: The most important piece, this is the heart of your Canon EOS R50. It houses the sensor and all the internal mechanisms that make the camera work.

- **Lens (if you bought a kit version)**: Often, Canon cameras come with a basic lens, such as the Canon RF-S 18-45mm or similar. For beginners, this is great for general photography.

- **Battery and Charger**: These power the camera, and the charger ensures you can recharge the battery when it runs low.

- **Strap**: The camera strap is essential for safely carrying the camera around your neck or shoulder, reducing the risk of accidental drops.

- **USB Cable**: This cable is used to connect the camera to your computer or other devices for transferring files.

- **User Manual and Warranty Cards**: Important for learning more about the camera and keeping track of your warranty.

- **Lens Caps and Body Cap**: These protect the sensor and lens from dust when not in use.

Each item is carefully packed in protective foam or plastic to prevent damage during transportation. Be sure to handle each component with care as you unbox them, especially the camera body and lens, to avoid any accidental damage.

2. Assembling the Camera

After unboxing, the next crucial step is assembling your Canon EOS R50, which involves attaching the lens, inserting the battery, and setting it up for the first use.

a) Attaching the Lens to the Camera Body

For most beginners, the first challenge is attaching the lens correctly. Here's a simple guide:

- **Remove the Body Cap and Lens Cap**:

    Start by removing the body cap from the camera and the rear lens cap from the lens. These caps protect the sensitive parts of the camera (the sensor) and the lens (the glass elements) from dust and scratches.

- **Align the Lens with the Camera Mount**:

On the Canon EOS R50, the camera body has an RF lens mount. There is usually a red or white alignment dot on both the lens and the camera body. Line up these dots to ensure you are positioning the lens correctly.

- **Secure the Lens**:

Once the lens is aligned with the mount, gently twist the lens in a clockwise direction until you hear a click. This click confirms that the lens is securely attached to the camera body. Always double-check that the lens is properly mounted before moving forward, as a loose lens can cause problems or even fall off.

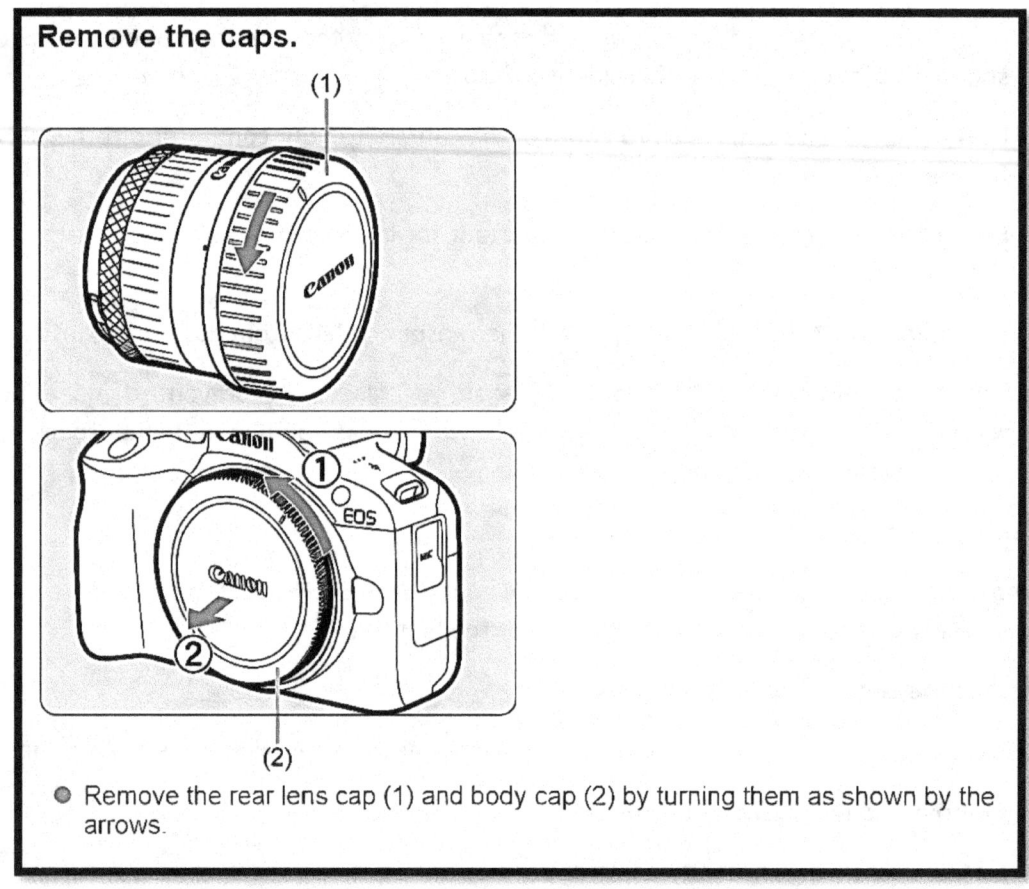

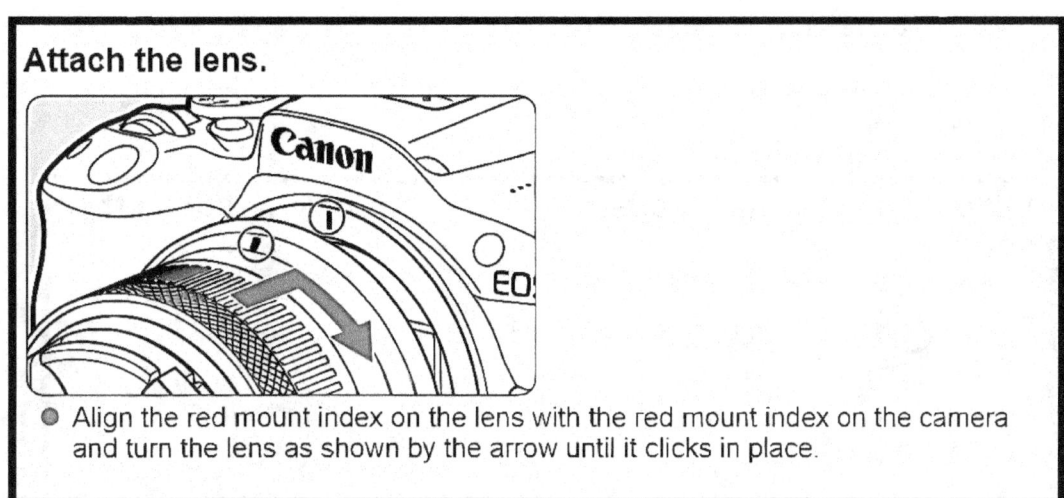

Attach the lens.

- Align the red mount index on the lens with the red mount index on the camera and turn the lens as shown by the arrow until it clicks in place.

Important Tip for Beginners: Avoid touching the glass on the lens or the sensor inside the camera body, as this can leave fingerprints or introduce dust, which can affect image quality.

b) Inserting the Battery and Memory Card

After attaching the lens, you'll need to power the camera by inserting the battery. Here's how you can do that:

- **Charge the Battery First**:

    Before inserting the battery into the camera, ensure it is fully charged using the provided charger. Typically, the battery will take a couple of hours to charge fully, and you'll notice an indicator light on the charger when it's ready.

- **Open the Battery Compartment**:

    On the bottom of the Canon EOS R50, you'll find a small door or latch labeled for the battery. Slide this open gently.

- **Insert the Battery**:

    The battery will only fit one way, so look for the battery's gold contacts and align them with the camera's contacts inside the compartment. Gently push the battery into place until you hear a soft click, indicating that it is secure.

- **Insert the Memory Card**:

    Alongside the battery compartment, there's usually a slot for the memory card (SD card). Insert the card with the label facing up and the metal contacts facing down. Again, push until it clicks into place.

- **Close the Battery Compartment:**

    Once both the battery and the memory card are inserted, close the compartment door, ensuring it clicks shut.

Slide the card/battery compartment cover lock and open the cover.

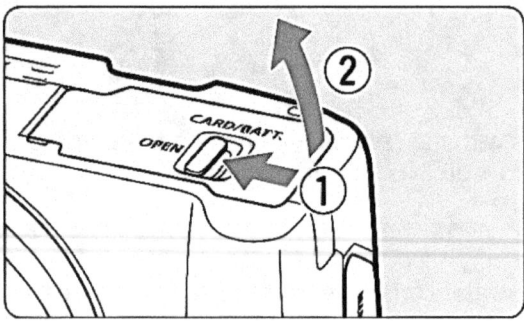

Insert the battery.

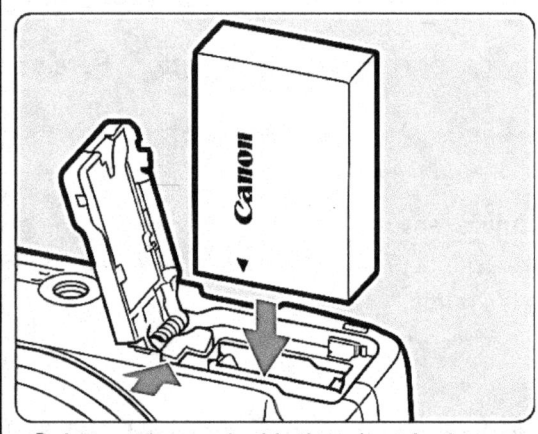

- Insert the end with the electrical contacts.
- Insert the battery until it locks in place.

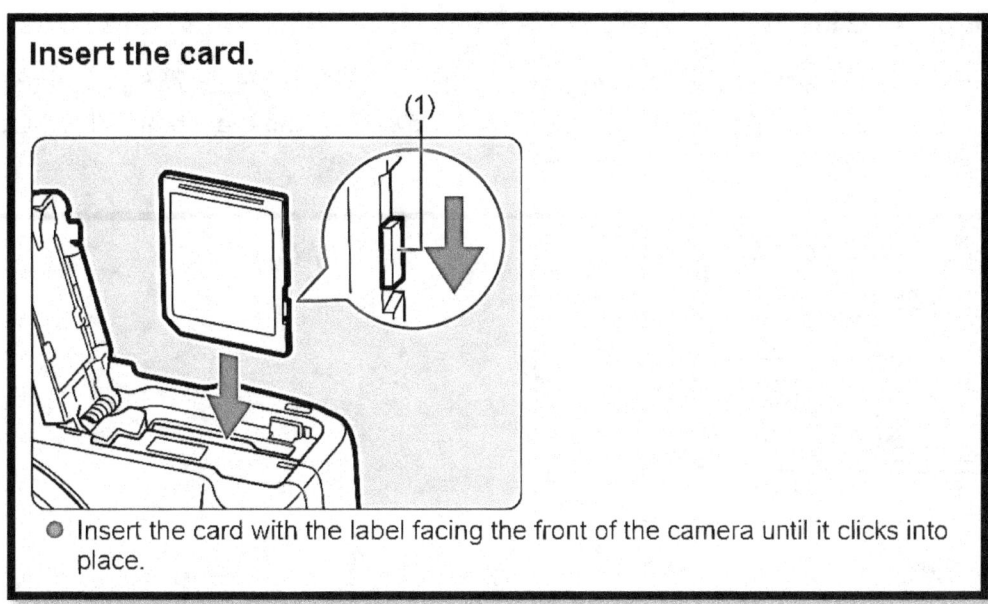

- Insert the card with the label facing the front of the camera until it clicks into place.

c) Attaching the Camera Strap

The camera strap is essential for both beginners and professionals. It helps prevent accidental drops and makes the camera easier to carry during long shoots.

- **Locate the Strap Mounts**:

    The Canon EOS R50 has two metal strap mounts, one on each side of the camera body.

- **Thread the Strap**:

    Take one end of the strap and thread it through the mount from the bottom. Once it's through the loop, thread the strap back through the plastic slider on the strap, adjusting it for length.

- **Secure the Strap**:

    Make sure the strap is tightly secured through the loops, so it won't slip out easily. Do the same for the other side.

Tip for Professionals: If you're working with heavier lenses or shooting for extended periods, consider investing in a padded strap for added comfort.

3. Powering Up the Camera for the First Time

With everything assembled, it's time to power on your Canon EOS R50 and make some initial adjustments.

a) Turning on the Camera

To turn on the Canon EOS R50, locate the power switch (usually on the top of the camera body) and toggle it to the "On" position. The camera should power up, and the screen will light up with the welcome menu.

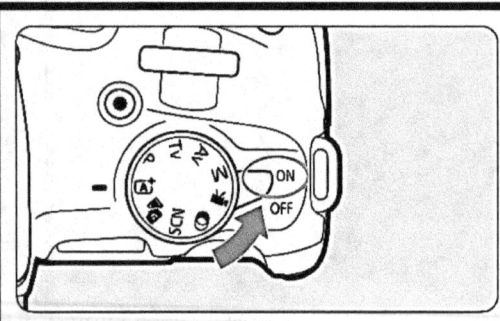

- **<ON>**
  The camera turns on. You can now shoot still photos and record movies.
- **<OFF>**
  The camera is turned off and does not function. Set the power switch to this position when not using the camera.

b) Initial Setup and Date/Time Settings

When turning on the camera for the first time, the Canon EOS R50 will prompt you to enter basic settings like date, time, and language. These steps are straightforward:

- **Language Selection**:

  Use the camera's touchscreen or dials to select your preferred language.

- **Date and Time Setup**:

  Set the date and time by tapping on the appropriate fields. Accurate date and time are important for timestamping your photos and videos.

- **Time Zone**:

  Choose the correct time zone for your location. This will help when traveling or syncing images across different devices.

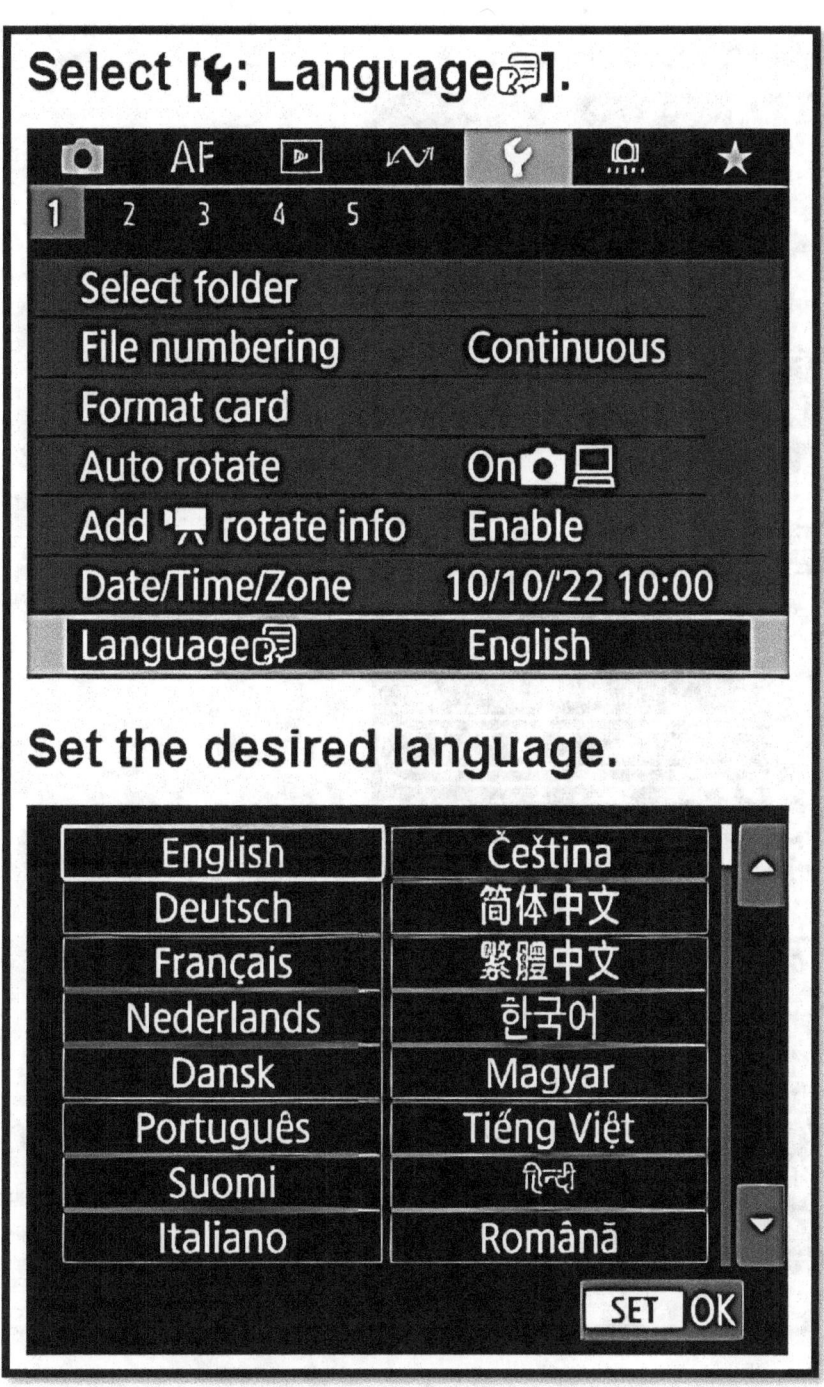

Select [🔧: Date/Time/Zone].

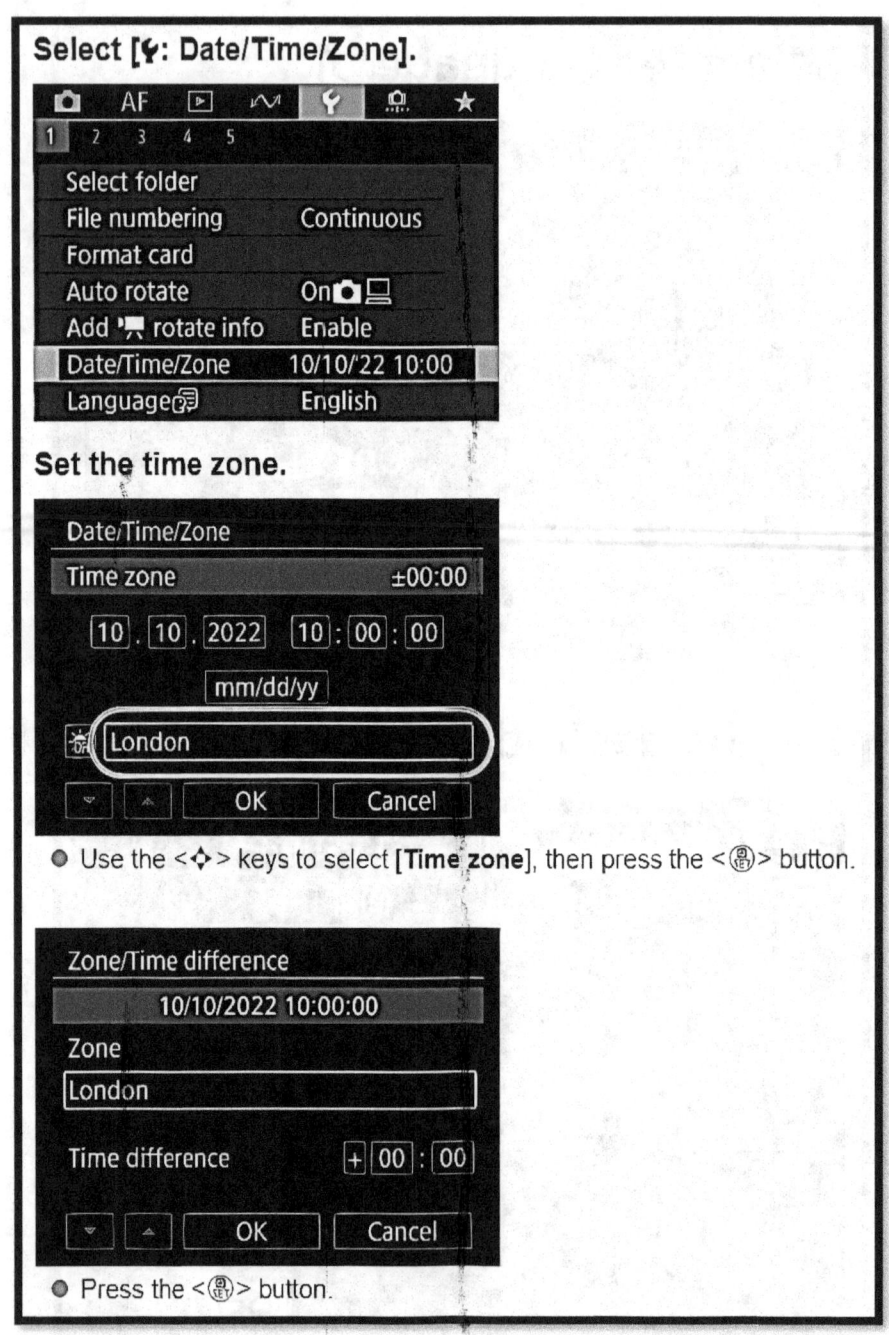

Set the time zone.

- Use the <✧> keys to select **[Time zone]**, then press the <⊛> button.

- Press the <⊛> button.

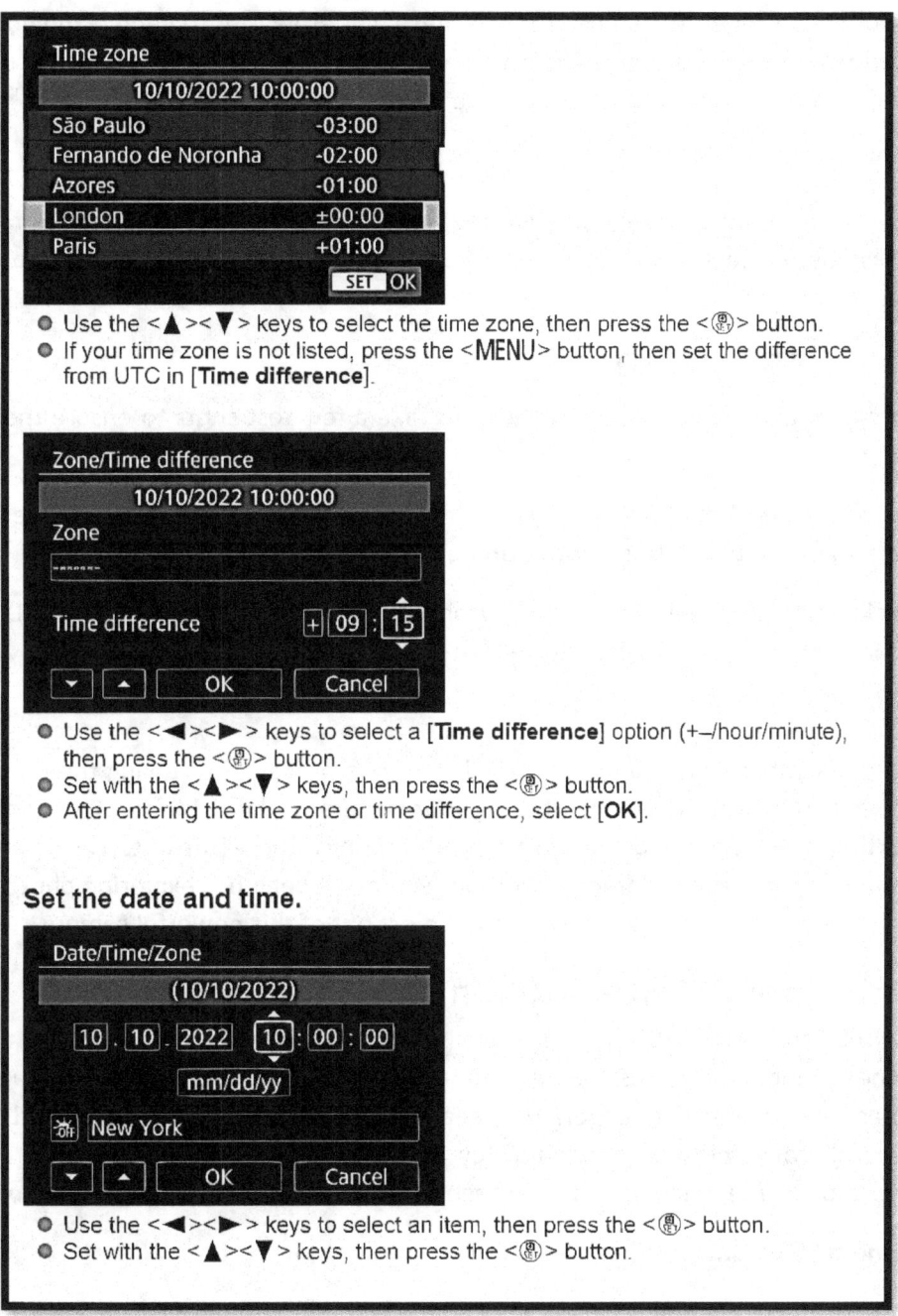

- Use the <▲><▼> keys to select the time zone, then press the <⊛> button.
- If your time zone is not listed, press the <MENU> button, then set the difference from UTC in [**Time difference**].

- Use the <◄><►> keys to select a [**Time difference**] option (+−/hour/minute), then press the <⊛> button.
- Set with the <▲><▼> keys, then press the <⊛> button.
- After entering the time zone or time difference, select [**OK**].

Set the date and time.

- Use the <◄><►> keys to select an item, then press the <⊛> button.
- Set with the <▲><▼> keys, then press the <⊛> button.

c) Image Quality and File Format

Before you start shooting, you might want to set your preferred image quality and file format:

- **RAW vs. JPEG**:

If you're a beginner, start with JPEG, as these files are easier to handle and don't require additional processing. However, if you're a professional looking for higher quality and more control in post-production, choose RAW.

- **File Size**:

Adjust the resolution based on your needs. For everyday shooting, a medium resolution works fine. Professionals may want to use the maximum resolution for more detailed images.

4. Final Check: Testing the Camera

Once everything is assembled, it's a good idea to take a few test shots to ensure the camera is working properly.

- **Test the Focus**: Aim at a subject and half-press the shutter button to test the autofocus. The camera should focus smoothly and quickly.

- **Check Image Preview**: After taking a photo, check the preview on the LCD screen to ensure everything is functioning well.

Conclusion

Unboxing and assembling the Canon EOS R50 is a simple process, but taking the time to follow each step carefully ensures that you start using your camera on the right foot. From attaching the lens to inserting the battery and customizing your settings, these early steps set the stage for successful photography or videography, whether you are a beginner exploring photography for the first time or a professional ready to make the most out of this powerful camera.

Basic Settings and Customization

Customizing the Canon EOS R50's basic settings is an important first step in ensuring the camera meets your needs and preferences. Customization allows you to tailor the camera's functionality, responsiveness, and overall user experience, enabling you to shoot comfortably and efficiently. This section will cover how to configure key camera settings, optimize exposure controls, customize autofocus (AF) functions, adjust image quality settings, and save personal presets.

1. Initial Camera Setup and Language Selection

Once you power on your Canon EOS R50, the camera will prompt you through a few initial setup steps, beginning with language selection. Choose your preferred language, then follow the prompts to set the date and time, which helps with organizing and timestamping photos.

Process:

- Power on the camera by flipping the switch located on the right side of the camera.

- Select your language from the list using the touchscreen or navigation buttons.
- Set the date, time, and time zone to keep your files organized chronologically.

2. Selecting Image Quality and File Format

Image quality settings on the Canon EOS R50 determine the size and detail level of each photo you capture. Beginners often start with JPEG format, which produces images that are already processed by the camera and ready for sharing. Professionals may prefer RAW files, which provide maximum image data for detailed post-processing.

Explanation:

- **JPEG**: Suitable for quick shots and social sharing. JPEG files are smaller and automatically processed by the camera for brightness, contrast, and sharpness.
- **RAW**: Recommended for professional editing. RAW files preserve all image data, giving you control over exposure, white balance, and detail adjustments during editing.

Process:

- Open the Menu, go to the "Image Quality" setting.
- Select either **RAW** for high-quality editing potential or **JPEG** for quick sharing, or **RAW + JPEG** if you want both versions saved.

3. Adjusting ISO Sensitivity for Low-Light Conditions

ISO sensitivity determines how your camera sensor responds to light, with lower values (like ISO 100) for bright settings and higher values (like ISO 3200) for low light. The Canon EOS R50 offers both an **Auto ISO** feature and manual ISO adjustments.

Explanation:

- **Auto ISO**: Convenient for beginners, as it automatically adjusts ISO based on lighting conditions.
- **Manual ISO**: For experienced photographers who want full control over light sensitivity.

Process:

- Press the **ISO button** or navigate to ISO settings in the Menu.
- Set ISO to **Auto** for ease, or select a specific ISO based on your shooting environment (ISO 100 for daylight, ISO 800+ for indoors or low light).

4. Setting the Autofocus Mode and Area Selection

The Canon EOS R50's autofocus system includes a variety of modes designed to suit different types of scenes and subjects. Mastering AF modes will make it easier to capture sharp images in diverse situations.

Explanation:

- **One-Shot AF**: Best for still subjects, locks focus when you half-press the shutter.
- **Servo AF**: Ideal for moving subjects, continuously adjusts focus as your subject moves.
- **Face/Eye Detection**: Automatically focuses on faces and eyes, a great feature for portraits.

Process:

- Access AF settings by pressing the **AF button** or going to the Menu.
- Choose **One-Shot AF** for stationary subjects, **Servo AF** for action shots, and **Face/Eye Detection** if you're photographing people.

5. Customizing Exposure Controls

The Canon EOS R50 provides various ways to control exposure, including setting aperture, shutter speed, and exposure compensation. Understanding these settings will help you capture images with the right brightness and creative effects.

Explanation:

- **Aperture** (f-stop): Controls the lens opening size and depth of field; lower f-numbers give a blurred background.
- **Shutter Speed**: Determines the duration the sensor is exposed to light; faster speeds (e.g., 1/1000) freeze action, while slower speeds (e.g., 1/30) blur motion.
- **Exposure Compensation**: Adjusts brightness without changing other settings.

Process:

- Set the **Aperture** using the **Control Dial** in Aperture Priority (Av) mode.
- Set **Shutter Speed** in Shutter Priority (Tv) mode.
- Use **Exposure Compensation** by pressing the Exposure button and turning the dial to make adjustments (negative values darken the image, positive values brighten it).

6. Configuring White Balance Settings

White balance adjusts the color temperature in your images, ensuring colors appear natural under different lighting conditions. The Canon EOS R50 offers preset white balance options, an Auto setting, and a Custom setting for professionals who need precise control.

Explanation:

- **Auto White Balance (AWB)**: The camera automatically corrects colors to look natural.
- **Preset Options**: Includes Daylight, Cloudy, Tungsten, etc., ideal for consistent lighting conditions.
- **Custom White Balance**: You can manually adjust for challenging lighting by setting the camera to a specific color temperature.

Process:

- Open the **White Balance Menu** from the Menu or Quick Menu.
- Choose **AWB** for automatic correction or **Preset Options** based on your lighting.
- For **Custom White Balance**, photograph a white card under the lighting you'll shoot in and set that photo as the reference.

7. Configuring Custom Buttons and Shortcuts

The Canon EOS R50 allows you to assign frequently used settings to specific buttons, making it quicker to access your favorite functions without navigating through menus.

Explanation:

- **Custom Buttons**: Assign actions like ISO, White Balance, or AF Mode to physical buttons.
- **Quick Menu**: Customize the Quick Menu to include your most-used functions.

Process:

- Go to **Menu > Custom Functions (C.Fn)**.
- Select **Customize Buttons**, then assign functions to your chosen buttons.
- Customize the **Quick Menu** by selecting functions you want quick access to during shoots.

8. Setting Up the Quick Control Dial and Touchscreen

Both the control dial and touchscreen allow you to navigate settings quickly. Understanding how to set them up will help you control your camera more efficiently.

Explanation:

- **Quick Control Dial**: Adjusts settings like exposure and aperture with a simple turn.
- **Touchscreen**: Enables tap-to-focus, menu navigation, and easy access to the Quick Menu.

Process:

- Access **Menu > Custom Functions (C.Fn)** to modify control dial functions.
- Enable **Touchscreen features** through the **Touch Control settings** in the Menu, allowing tap-to-focus and swipe navigation.

9. Saving Your Custom Settings

After setting up the Canon EOS R50 according to your preferences, you can save these settings for easy recall in different shooting situations.

Explanation:

- **User Presets**: Allows you to save custom settings, so you don't have to reconfigure them each time you start a new shoot.

Process:

- Go to **Menu > Custom Shooting Mode (C1, C2, C3)**.
- Select **Register Settings** and save your current configuration.

10. Resetting the Camera to Factory Settings

If you need to start over, you can reset the camera to its original settings. This is useful when troubleshooting or if you want to return to the default configuration.

Process:

- Open the **Menu** and go to **Clear Settings**.
- Choose **Reset Camera** to revert to factory settings.

Conclusion

In this section, you've learned how to customize your Canon EOS R50's basic settings to suit your shooting style, maximize functionality, and streamline your experience.

Firmware Updates and Camera Maintenance

Updating your camera's firmware and performing regular maintenance are vital for ensuring optimal performance, expanding your camera's functionality, and prolonging its life. Firmware updates introduce new features, improve performance, and sometimes fix minor bugs, while regular maintenance keeps the camera's hardware in top shape. This section will explain why and how to update firmware, and provide essential maintenance tips for keeping your Canon EOS R50 in excellent condition.

1. Understanding Firmware and Its Importance

Firmware is the internal software that controls the camera's functions and interface. Canon periodically releases firmware updates to enhance the camera's performance, add new features, and fix software bugs. Updating firmware is like giving your camera a small "tune-up" to ensure it's performing with the latest advancements.

Explanation:

- **Firmware** controls everything from autofocus responsiveness to how the camera communicates with external devices.
- **Benefits of Firmware Updates**: New firmware may improve autofocus speed, add new shooting features, enhance connectivity options, and resolve minor operational issues.

2. Checking for Firmware Updates

To ensure your camera is always up-to-date, you should periodically check for new firmware updates. Canon posts firmware updates on its official website, and checking is quick and easy. It's advisable to check for updates every few months or whenever you notice a new feature you're interested in.

Process:

- **Go to Canon's website** (specific to your region) and search for the Canon EOS R50 under the Support section.
- **Download the Latest Firmware** if available, making sure it matches your camera model (Canon EOS R50) to avoid compatibility issues.
- **Prepare an SD Card**: You'll need an SD card to transfer the firmware file to the camera.

3. Preparing to Install Firmware Updates

Before installing firmware, ensure your camera is fully charged or connected to a power source. An interruption during the update could cause issues, so it's essential to have a reliable power source and a properly formatted SD card.

Preparation Steps:

- **Charge the Battery** to at least 75% or use an AC adapter if available.

- **Format an SD Card** within the camera itself to clear any previous data that might interfere with the update.
- **Transfer the Firmware File**: Move the downloaded firmware file from your computer to the formatted SD card.

4. Installing the Firmware Update

Once the firmware file is on the SD card, you're ready to install the update. The camera's Menu has a dedicated firmware update option that guides you through the process.

Process:

- Insert the **SD card with the firmware file** into the camera.
- Go to the **Menu > Firmware Version** and select **Update**.
- Follow the on-screen instructions, which typically include prompts to confirm the update. Avoid touching the camera or turning it off during the update process.
- Wait for the camera to complete the update, and restart it if prompted.

5. Verifying the Firmware Update

After installation, verify that the update was successful by checking the firmware version number. This ensures that the camera is now running the latest software.

Process:

- Go to **Menu > Firmware Version** to view the installed version.
- Confirm that the version number matches the latest update. If it does, the firmware update was successful; if not, try reinstalling or consult Canon support for guidance.

6. Basic Maintenance: Keeping Your Camera Clean

A well-maintained camera not only lasts longer but also provides consistent image quality. Dust, fingerprints, and moisture can affect image quality and camera performance, so cleaning should be a regular practice.

Explanation:

- **Lens Cleaning**: Dust or smudges on the lens can degrade image sharpness and clarity.
- **Sensor Cleaning**: Even though the EOS R50 has a sensor cleaning function, occasional manual cleaning may be necessary in dusty environments.

- **Body Cleaning**: The camera's exterior should also be cleaned to remove dust and grime, especially around buttons and dials.

Process:

- **Lens**: Use a microfiber cloth to gently wipe the lens. For deeper cleaning, use lens cleaner fluid or a blower brush.
- **Sensor**: The EOS R50 has an automatic sensor cleaning function. For stubborn dust spots, you may need to use a sensor swab.
- **Body**: Wipe the camera body with a soft, lint-free cloth, paying attention to button crevices.

7. Protecting the Sensor and Lens from Dust and Debris

Changing lenses introduces the risk of dust entering the camera body, which can settle on the sensor. When possible, avoid changing lenses in windy or dusty environments, and follow specific precautions to protect the camera's internal components.

Precautions:

- **Turn off the camera** before switching lenses to reduce static electricity that can attract dust.
- **Hold the camera body downward** while changing lenses to minimize exposure.
- **Use lens caps** when the lens is not attached to the camera.

8. Storing the Camera and Battery Maintenance

Proper storage is essential for preventing damage from humidity, dust, and temperature extremes. Battery maintenance also prolongs battery life and ensures the camera is ready when you need it.

Storage Tips:

- **Use a camera bag** that provides padding and protects from dust and moisture.
- **Avoid high heat or humidity**, which can damage the electronics and lens elements.
- **Remove the battery** if the camera won't be used for an extended period, and store it in a cool, dry place.

Battery Care:

- Recharge your battery regularly, even if the camera is not in use.

- Avoid letting the battery drain completely, as this can reduce its lifespan over time.
- Use only Canon-approved batteries to ensure compatibility and safety.

9. Performing a Regular Function Check

Running a quick function check every few months is a good way to ensure your Canon EOS R50 is operating smoothly. This involves testing key features to confirm they're functioning correctly, helping catch issues before they affect a shoot.

Function Check Process:

- **Power On and Test Shutter**: Confirm the camera powers on smoothly and that the shutter responds.
- **Test Autofocus**: Confirm autofocus modes work correctly in different settings.
- **Check the Menu**: Navigate the menu and test essential functions like exposure adjustments and playback to ensure all controls respond correctly.

10. Troubleshooting Common Issues

Even with regular maintenance, you may encounter occasional issues. Knowing how to troubleshoot these common problems will save time and potentially avoid repair costs.

Common Issues and Fixes:

- **Camera Won't Power On**: Check the battery level, and ensure the battery is inserted correctly. If the issue persists, try using a different, fully charged battery.
- **Autofocus Not Responding**: Ensure the lens AF switch is set to AF, not MF (manual focus), and clean the lens contacts.
- **Unresponsive Buttons**: Turn the camera off and back on. If the problem continues, try resetting the camera settings to factory defaults via the Menu.

11. Firmware Updates for Lenses and Accessories

In addition to the camera itself, some lenses and accessories require firmware updates to ensure compatibility and performance improvements. Keeping these accessories up-to-date will help you maximize the performance of the Canon EOS R50.

Explanation:

- Some Canon lenses and external accessories (e.g., flash units) may have their own firmware updates, which can be installed through the camera or using Canon's software on a computer.

Process:

- **Check for Lens Firmware**: Go to Canon's website or connect your camera to Canon's software to check for updates.
- **Install Lens Firmware**: Insert the SD card with the firmware file and follow the on-screen instructions in the camera's Menu.

Conclusion

Keeping your Canon EOS R50 updated and properly maintained is essential for ensuring it performs well over time. By following the firmware update process and implementing a regular maintenance routine, you'll keep your camera in peak condition, enhance its capabilities, and prevent common issues that can arise with prolonged use. Remember, a well-maintained camera not only enhances your experience as a photographer but also extends the lifespan of your equipment, making it a reliable tool for capturing your creative vision.

CHAPTER 3

NAVIGATING THE CAMERA'S INTERFACE

Buttons, Dials, and Touchscreen Controls

The Canon EOS R50 is designed with an intuitive interface, making it approachable for beginners while providing plenty of depth for experienced photographers. In this section, we'll explore the camera's physical buttons, dials, and its touchscreen controls, which collectively allow you to operate the camera and customize its functions to your preference.

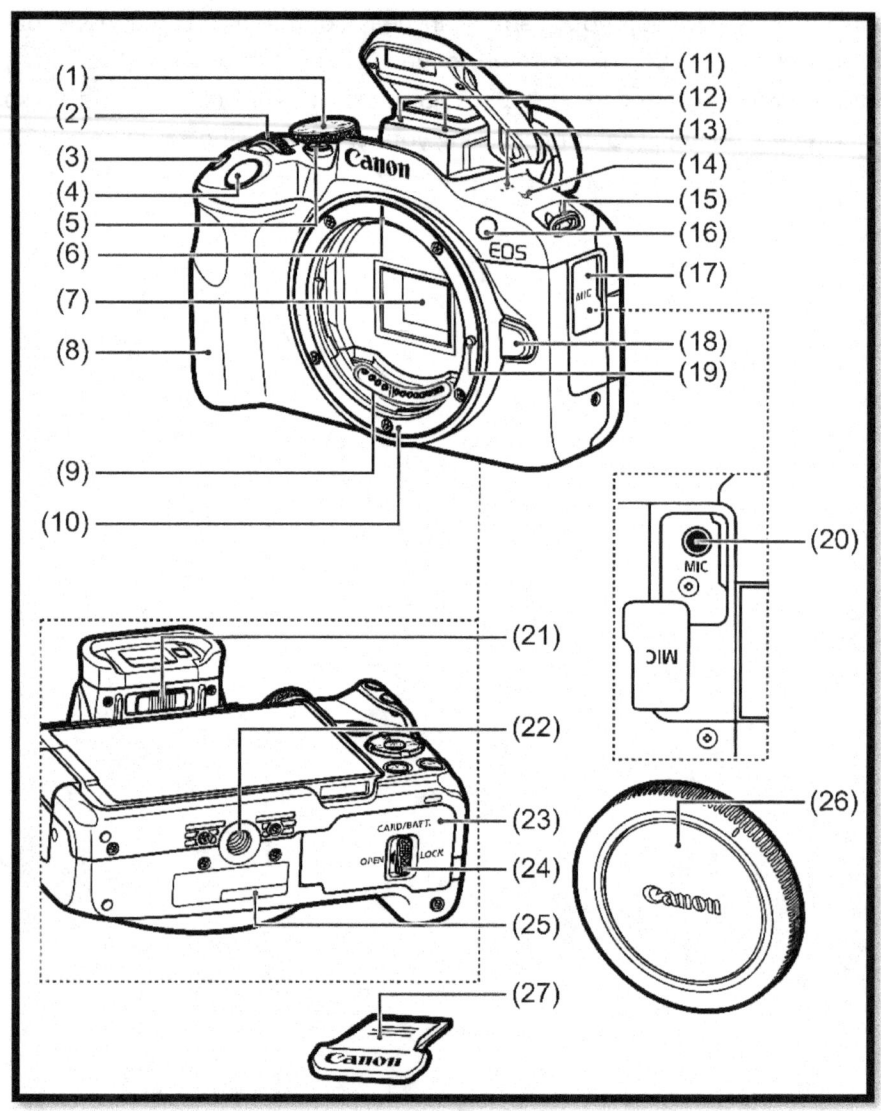

(1)	Mode dial	(15)	Strap mount
(2)	<☼> Dial	(16)	AF-assist beam/red-eye reduction/self-timer/remote control lamp
(3)	<ISO> ISO speed setting button		
(4)	Shutter button	(17)	Terminal cover
(5)	Movie shooting button	(18)	Lens release button
(6)	RF lens mount index	(19)	Lens lock pin
(7)	Image sensor	(20)	<MIC> External microphone IN terminal
(8)	Grip		
(9)	Contacts	(21)	Dioptric adjustment slider
(10)	Lens mount	(22)	Tripod socket
(11)	Built-in flash	(23)	Card/battery compartment cover
(12)	Microphone	(24)	Card/battery compartment cover lock
(13)	Speaker		
(14)	<⊖> Focal plane mark	(25)	Serial number (body number)
		(26)	Body cap
		(27)	Shoe cover

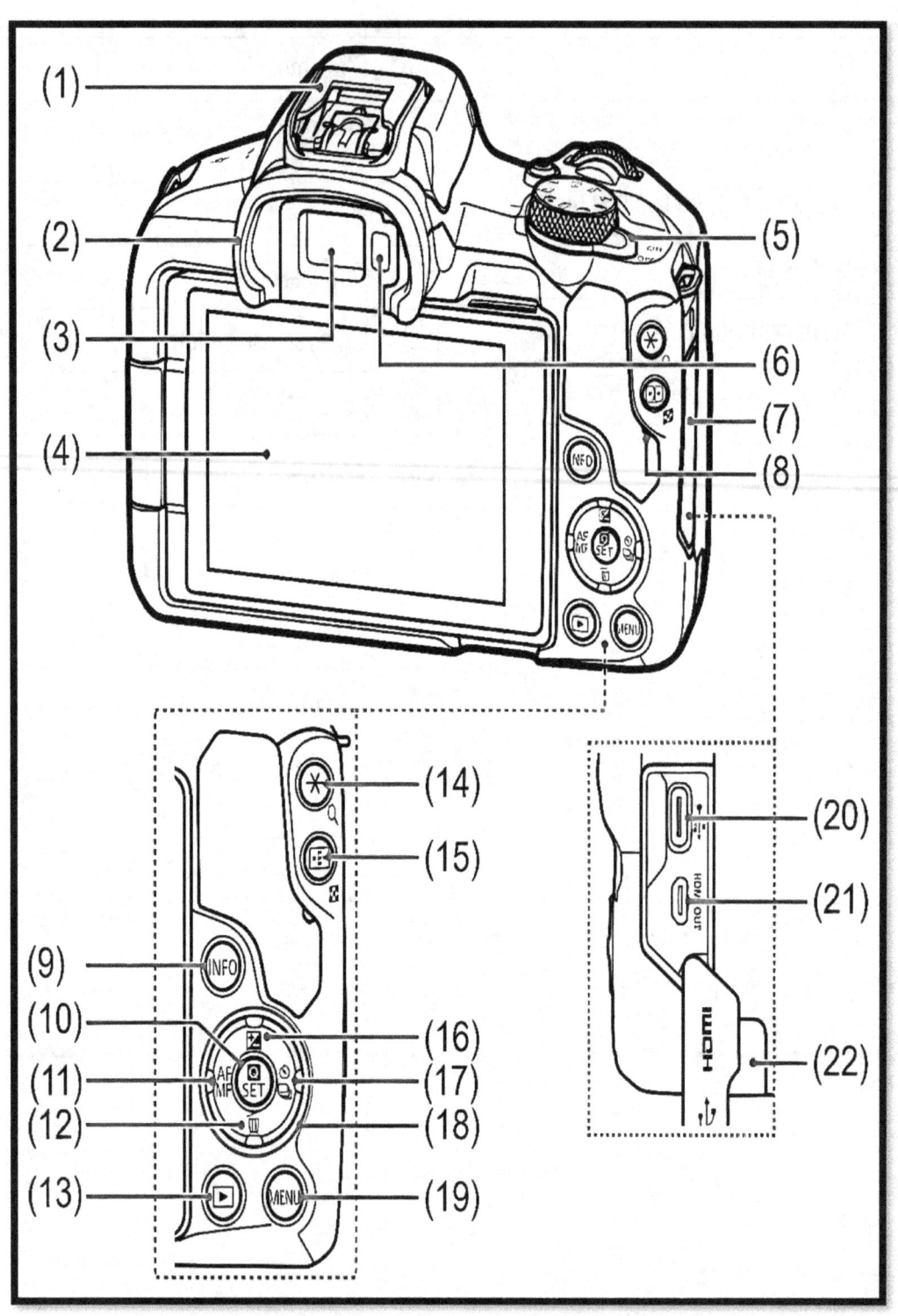

(1)	Multi-function shoe	(12)	<▼/🗑> Down/erase button
(2)	Eyecup	(13)	<▶> Playback button
(3)	Viewfinder eyepiece	(14)	<✱/🔍> AE lock/FE lock/magnify button
(4)	Screen		
(5)	<ON/OFF> Power switch	(15)	<⊞/⊡> AF point selection/index/reduce button
(6)	Viewfinder sensor		
(7)	Terminal cover	(16)	<▲/⚖> Up/exposure compensation button
(8)	Access lamp		
(9)	<INFO> Info button	(17)	<▶/⏱/⏵> Right/self-timer/drive mode selection button
(10)	<⊛> Quick Control/Set button		
(11)	<◀/AF MF> Left/autofocus/manual focus button	(18)	<✧> Cross keys
		(19)	<MENU> Menu button
		(20)	<⇌> Digital terminal
		(21)	<HDMI OUT> HDMI micro OUT terminal
		(22)	DC cord hole

Overview: Understanding Your Camera's Interface

The Canon EOS R50's controls fall into three main categories:

1. **Buttons** – Used for specific tasks like accessing menus, focusing, and taking photos.

2. **Dials** – Primarily for adjusting settings such as shutter speed, aperture, and other exposure values.

3. **Touchscreen Controls** – An interactive screen that lets you tap, swipe, and adjust settings directly.

Each of these components allows you to navigate, customize, and use the camera efficiently. By mastering these controls, you'll have the flexibility to take full creative control over your images.

1. Buttons: Your Camera's Primary Controls

Buttons on the Canon EOS R50 provide quick access to essential camera functions. They are thoughtfully laid out to enable fast adjustments, even when you're shooting on the go. Let's go over some of the main buttons:

a) Shutter Button

The shutter button is likely the most important button on your camera, as it's what you press to take a photo. Located on the top right side of the camera, this button has a two-step process:

- **Half-press** the button to focus. You'll feel a slight resistance halfway down. This action triggers the autofocus, allowing the camera to focus on your subject.
- **Full-press** the button to take the photo. Pressing down fully captures the image.

For beginners, practice holding the button halfway first to see how the camera focuses before snapping the shot.

b) Power Button

The power button is also located on the top of the camera. It has a simple toggle for switching the camera **on** or **off**. Turn it off when the camera is not in use to conserve battery life.

c) Mode Button

The mode button lets you switch between shooting modes, such as **Manual**, **Aperture Priority**, and **Shutter Priority** modes. Pressing this button displays the available modes on the screen. For beginners, this is a key control to familiarize yourself with, as it allows you to select modes based on different shooting needs, like portraits or action shots.

d) Playback Button

The playback button allows you to view photos and videos you've already taken. This button is typically marked with a triangular "Play" icon and is usually located near the screen. Pressing it brings up your last shot, and you can use the touchscreen to scroll through your images.

e) Menu Button

The menu button opens up the camera's main menu, where you'll find in-depth settings for customizing your camera. It's a critical button for accessing advanced settings, but it's also where you'll adjust basic preferences, such as image quality and white balance.

f) Info Button

The info button displays additional information about the current camera settings on the screen. Pressing it cycles through different display options, which can show anything from exposure settings to a histogram for evaluating image brightness.

g) AF-On Button (Back Button Focus)

For more advanced users, the AF-On button enables back-button focusing. This method separates focusing from the shutter button, giving you more control over focus without accidentally capturing an image. It's useful in dynamic environments where you need quick, repetitive focus adjustments.

2. Dials: Adjusting Key Camera Settings

Dials on the Canon EOS R50 allow you to quickly control essential settings like shutter speed, aperture, and ISO. Knowing how to use the dials will speed up your shooting process and enable you to react quickly to changing light conditions or subject movement.

a) Main Control Dial

The main control dial is located near the shutter button, making it easy to adjust with your index finger. Depending on the shooting mode, this dial adjusts different settings:

- In **Manual Mode**, it adjusts the shutter speed.
- In **Aperture Priority Mode (Av)**, it adjusts the aperture.
- In **Shutter Priority Mode (Tv)**, it sets the shutter speed.

This control dial is essential for photographers who prefer manual control over exposure settings. Beginners should experiment with this dial in different modes to understand how it affects the image.

b) Quick Control Dial

The quick control dial is usually located on the back of the camera, within easy reach of your thumb. It lets you navigate settings in the Quick Menu, making it easy to change settings without diving into the main menu.

c) Exposure Compensation Dial

Although this dial might not be a standalone control, the exposure compensation feature is accessible through the main control dial when in certain shooting modes, such as **Aperture Priority**. Use it to brighten or darken your image based on the camera's current exposure settings. Beginners can use this feature to correct images when they look too dark or too bright.

3. Touchscreen Controls: Modern, Intuitive Interface

One of the standout features of the Canon EOS R50 is its fully responsive touchscreen. This is especially helpful for beginners, as it provides an intuitive way to interact with the camera's settings and features.

a) Touch to Focus

The touchscreen allows you to tap directly on the area of the screen where you want the camera to focus. This is particularly helpful in situations where you want to quickly change your focus point, such as when photographing a subject that's not centered in the frame.

To enable touch focus:

> Tap on the **AF** area on the screen, and the camera will adjust focus to that spot.

b) Touch Shutter

With the touch shutter feature, you can take a photo by simply tapping on the screen. This is useful for self-portraits or shots where you want to avoid camera shake from pressing the shutter button.

To activate touch shutter:

- Locate the **Touch Shutter** icon on the screen, usually represented by a small camera icon.
- Tap the icon to turn on this function, and tap anywhere on the screen to capture a photo.

c) Quick Menu (Q Menu)

The Quick Menu offers a simplified interface for accessing frequently used settings without going into the main menu. You can open the Quick Menu by pressing the **Q** button or by tapping the **Q** icon on the screen. Here, you can adjust settings such as white balance, ISO, and picture style with just a few taps.

For beginners, this menu is a great way to get comfortable adjusting essential settings without feeling overwhelmed.

d) Swiping and Pinching for Playback

In playback mode, you can use familiar gestures like swiping and pinching to view your images. Swiping left or right moves through images, while pinching in or out lets you zoom in or out. This makes reviewing images easy, and you can quickly check details in the photo, such as sharpness or focus accuracy.

e) Settings and Menu Navigation

The touchscreen also allows you to navigate the main menu and change settings directly. This is especially helpful for new users who find it easier to select options by tapping rather than using buttons or dials.

To access the menu:

- Press the **Menu** button to bring up the options on the touchscreen.
- You can then tap through each setting category and make adjustments.

f) Playback and Delete Options

When viewing images, you can delete unwanted photos by tapping the trash icon. This is a quick way to manage your storage without having to go through detailed menu settings.

For beginners, it's useful to delete images that didn't turn out well to keep storage space open for new shots.

Conclusion

Mastering the buttons, dials, and touchscreen controls on the Canon EOS R50 will transform your shooting experience. By understanding each of these elements, you'll be able to control your camera efficiently, making you ready for any shooting situation. Remember to experiment with each control to find the configuration that best suits your style, and over time, you'll find yourself navigating the camera's interface with ease and confidence.

Menu System Overview

The Canon EOS R50 offers a comprehensive menu system that allows you to control nearly every aspect of the camera's operation. While the range of options might seem overwhelming at first, breaking it down into manageable sections makes it easier to understand. This menu system is designed for flexibility, allowing both beginners and professionals to adjust the camera settings to their needs. In this chapter, we'll explore the menu layout, each major menu section, and key settings within each section.

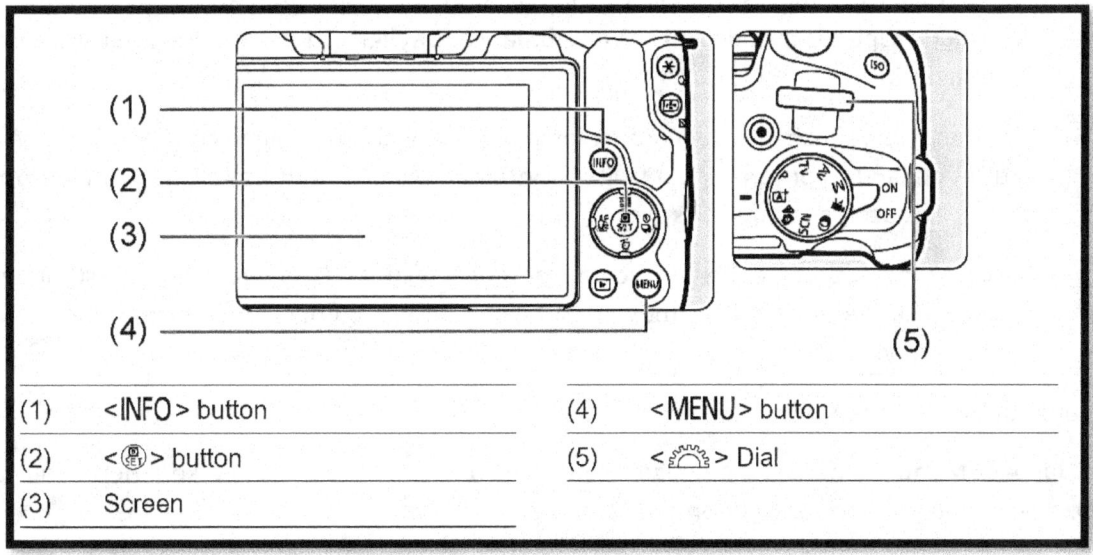

(1)	<INFO> button	(4)	<MENU> button
(2)	<⊕> button	(5)	<⚙> Dial
(3)	Screen		

Understanding the Basic Layout of the Menu

The menu is organized into categories that are color-coded for easy navigation. Each category contains multiple settings pages, which makes it easier to find specific options without scrolling through a long list. Here's how to access and navigate the menu system:

1. **Accessing the Menu**: Press the **Menu** button on the back of the camera. This opens up the main menu screen.
2. **Navigating**: Use the arrow keys, control dial, or touchscreen to move through each category and select items.
3. **Selecting an Option**: Once you highlight a setting, press the **Set** button or tap the option on the screen if touchscreen control is enabled.
4. **Returning to Shooting Mode**: Press the **Shutter** button halfway down to exit the menu and return to shooting.

1. Shooting Menu (Red Tab)

The **Shooting Menu** contains settings related to image capture, including options for image quality, focus, and shooting modes.

Key Settings in the Shooting Menu

- **Image Quality**: Allows you to choose between different file formats, such as **RAW** and **JPEG**, and adjust the resolution. RAW files offer maximum detail and flexibility for editing, while JPEG files are smaller and ready for immediate use.
- **White Balance**: Adjusts the color temperature of your images based on lighting conditions. Options include **Auto White Balance**, **Daylight**, **Tungsten**, **Fluorescent**, and a custom option.
- **Picture Style**: Adjusts the appearance of your photos by controlling contrast, sharpness, saturation, and color tone. Presets like **Standard**, **Portrait**, **Landscape**, and **Monochrome** allow quick access to popular styles.
- **Focus Mode**: Controls the autofocus method, such as **One-Shot AF** (for stationary subjects) or **Servo AF** (for moving subjects). It's an important setting for action photography.

2. Playback Menu (Blue Tab)

The **Playback Menu** is where you manage photos and videos you've already taken. Here, you can view, delete, and edit images right on the camera.

Key Settings in the Playback Menu

- **Image Review**: Sets how long the image appears on the screen after taking a shot. Options include showing the image for 2 seconds, 4 seconds, or keeping it off entirely.

- **Protect Images**: Allows you to mark images as "protected," which prevents them from being accidentally deleted.

- **Rotate Image**: Provides a way to rotate images for correct orientation on the camera display.

- **Slide Show**: Creates a slideshow of your photos with custom display intervals.

- **RAW Processing**: Allows basic edits to RAW images within the camera, such as adjusting brightness and white balance before saving as JPEGs.

3. Setup Menu (Yellow Tab)

The **Setup Menu** includes options for configuring the camera's general settings, such as date and time, file numbering, and screen brightness.

Key Settings in the Setup Menu

- **Date/Time**: Set or update the camera's internal clock, which is critical for accurate timestamps on your photos.

- **Language**: Select your preferred language for the menu display.

- **Video System**: Adjusts the display standard to **NTSC** or **PAL** based on your region.

- **File Numbering**: Determines whether the camera resets file numbering or continues from the last file. Continuous numbering is ideal for organizing photos.

- **Screen Brightness**: Adjusts the brightness of the LCD screen. Increasing brightness can help in bright conditions, while lowering it can conserve battery life.

- **Battery Info**: Displays battery charge and health status, which helps you gauge battery life during a shoot.

4. Custom Function Menu (Orange Tab)

The **Custom Function Menu** is a powerful section that allows more experienced photographers to personalize camera functions, providing more control over how the camera responds in various shooting conditions.

Key Settings in the Custom Function Menu

- **Custom Buttons**: Assign specific functions to different buttons on the camera for faster access. For example, you could set the **AF-On** button for back-button focusing.
- **Dial Function**: Adjusts the behavior of the camera's dials, such as reversing the control directions.
- **Exposure Level Increments**: Sets the increment levels for exposure adjustments. Choose between 1/3-stop or 1/2-stop increments based on your preference.
- **AF-Assist Beam Firing**: Allows you to control whether the autofocus assist light is used in low light situations.

5. My Menu (Green Tab)

The **My Menu** tab is a customizable section where you can add your most frequently used settings for quick access. This is especially useful for photographers who frequently adjust specific settings.

Key Settings in My Menu

- **Add/Delete Items**: Customize this menu by adding or removing specific settings from other menu sections. For instance, if you often adjust white balance, you can add it here for easy access.
- **Sort Items**: Organize items in your preferred order.
- **Display from My Menu**: Set this option to open My Menu as the default menu screen whenever you press the Menu button.

Practical Guide: Accessing Key Features in the Menu System

For both beginners and professionals, navigating through the various menu options quickly becomes second nature with practice. Below are steps to help guide new users through a few common tasks in the menu:

1. **Setting the Image Quality**:
   - Press the **Menu** button to access the main menu.
   - Navigate to the **Shooting Menu** (Red Tab).
   - Find and select **Image Quality**. Use the control dial to select between RAW, JPEG, or both. Beginners might find JPEG more convenient for quick sharing, while professionals may prefer RAW for detailed editing.

2. **Customizing White Balance**:
   - In the **Shooting Menu**, find **White Balance**.

- Choose a preset, like **Auto White Balance** or **Daylight**, or set a custom white balance by taking a photo of a neutral object (like a white sheet of paper) under current lighting conditions.
- Press **Set** to confirm.

3. **Creating a My Menu Tab for Quick Access**:

   - Go to the **My Menu** (Green Tab).
   - Select **Add Items** and choose commonly adjusted settings, such as **ISO** or **Metering Mode**.
   - Once added, return to **Sort Items** to organize them based on your shooting workflow.
   - By setting **Display from My Menu** to **Enable**, this section will open first when you press the Menu button.

4. **Adjusting Screen Brightness**:

   - Go to the **Setup Menu** (Yellow Tab).
   - Find and select **Screen Brightness**.
   - Adjust the brightness level to suit your environment, particularly useful when shooting outdoors in bright sunlight or in low light.

5. **Setting Continuous File Numbering**:

   - Access the **Setup Menu** (Yellow Tab).
   - Select **File Numbering** and set it to **Continuous** if you'd like file numbering to resume from the last shot. This feature is helpful for photographers who manage large batches of images and want a sequential file order.

Conclusion

The Canon EOS R50's menu system provides all the essential tools needed to fine-tune and personalize your camera settings. While the options may seem numerous, familiarizing yourself with these menus allows you to unlock the full potential of the camera. The more you navigate and use these settings, the more efficiently you'll be able to set up your camera for any shooting situation. Practicing with these menu options will not only build your confidence in operating the camera but will also enhance your overall shooting experience.

Customizing Function Buttons and Shortcuts

The Canon EOS R50 offers several customizable function buttons and shortcuts that allow you to streamline your workflow. By assigning frequently used functions to specific buttons, you can access important settings instantly, which is especially valuable in fast-paced shooting situations.

Whether you're a beginner looking to keep things simple or a professional wanting to work efficiently, customizing these buttons will help you gain full control of your camera.

In this section, we'll walk through the key function buttons and shortcuts on the Canon EOS R50, explain their default settings, and guide you in setting them up to fit your needs.

1. Overview of Customizable Buttons and Shortcuts

The Canon EOS R50 provides several customizable buttons, allowing you to change their functions. These buttons typically include:

- **AF-ON Button**: Located on the back, often used for back-button focusing.
- **Multi-Function (M-Fn) Button**: Found on the top of the camera, providing quick access to a range of settings.
- **Set Button**: Located in the center of the control dial, this button can be customized for various tasks.
- **Touchscreen Shortcuts**: Accessible via the Quick Control Menu, allowing you to tap directly on the screen to adjust certain settings.

Each of these buttons can be assigned a specific function, such as changing ISO, adjusting white balance, or accessing focus modes. This means that once set up, you won't need to navigate the main menu to make these adjustments, saving valuable time.

2. Understanding Button Customization Options

When customizing buttons, you'll find a wide range of options in the menu, including:

- **ISO**: Controls the camera's sensitivity to light.
- **White Balance**: Adjusts color temperature for different lighting conditions.
- **Autofocus Mode**: Switches between autofocus modes like **One-Shot AF** or **Servo AF**.
- **Drive Mode**: Allows you to switch between single shooting, burst shooting, and self-timer.
- **Exposure Compensation**: Adjusts brightness by adding or subtracting light.

Selecting functions that you adjust frequently as your shortcuts will streamline your shooting experience. For example, if you frequently shoot in varying light conditions, setting a button for ISO or White Balance adjustments can help you respond quickly.

3. Step-by-Step Guide to Customizing Buttons

Customizing function buttons on the Canon EOS R50 is simple and can be done through the menu. Let's go through the steps to customize each button:

a) AF-ON Button Customization

The **AF-ON** button is usually dedicated to back-button focusing, separating focusing from the shutter release. This can be useful in situations where you want to maintain focus on a specific point without capturing an image each time.

- **Access the Menu**: Press the **Menu** button to open the main menu.
- **Navigate to the Custom Functions (C.Fn) Menu**: Look for the orange tab labeled **C.Fn** for customization options.
- **Select Custom Buttons**: Choose the **AF-ON** button from the list.
- **Choose Your Function**: You'll see a list of options, including **Metering and AF Start**, **One-Shot AF**, **Exposure Lock**, and more. Select **Metering and AF Start** for traditional back-button focusing.

b) Multi-Function (M-Fn) Button Customization

The **M-Fn** button provides access to multiple functions at the press of a button, including ISO, drive mode, and exposure compensation.

- **Open the Menu**: Press **Menu** to access settings.
- **Navigate to Custom Functions**: Find the **C.Fn** tab.
- **Select the M-Fn Button**: Choose **M-Fn** from the custom buttons list.
- **Assign a Shortcut**: Options may include **ISO Speed Settings**, **Exposure Compensation**, or **White Balance**. For example, if you set it to **ISO Speed Settings**, you can adjust ISO quickly by pressing **M-Fn** and rotating the main control dial.

c) Set Button Customization

The **Set** button, located at the center of the control dial, can be assigned a specific function to streamline common adjustments.

- **Access Custom Button Settings**: Go to the Custom Functions menu in the **C.Fn** tab.
- **Select Set Button**: Choose the **Set** button from the list.

- **Choose Your Function**: You could set this button to **ISO, Exposure Compensation**, or **White Balance**. Selecting **Exposure Compensation**, for instance, allows quick adjustments for brightness correction.

4. Utilizing the Quick Control Menu for Touchscreen Shortcuts

In addition to physical buttons, the Canon EOS R50's **Quick Control Menu** (Q Menu) provides customizable touchscreen shortcuts. This feature allows you to access essential settings with a tap, providing a convenient alternative to physical buttons.

Steps to Customize the Q Menu

- **Press the Q Button**: This opens the Quick Control Menu on the touchscreen.
- **Tap and Hold a Setting**: Press and hold any setting to open the customization options.
- **Select Your Preferred Settings**: Replace default items with settings you use frequently, such as ISO, white balance, or focus mode.
- **Save Your Configuration**: Once you've customized your Q Menu, the changes will stay in place, giving you instant access to your chosen settings during a shoot.

This method of customization is great for beginners, as it provides visual access to key settings without needing to memorize button functions.

5. Best Practices for Button and Shortcut Customization

To make the most of button and shortcut customization, consider these best practices:

- **Identify Your Needs**: Think about the adjustments you make most often. If you frequently change ISO or white balance, prioritize those functions for customization.
- **Start Simple**: For beginners, it may be best to assign just one or two buttons at first, gradually adding more as you become comfortable with the camera.
- **Match Settings to Shooting Styles**: Professionals shooting action scenes may benefit from quick access to **AF Mode** and **Drive Mode**, while landscape photographers may want easy access to **Exposure Compensation** and **ISO**.
- **Practice and Adjust**: Customization is all about efficiency, so don't hesitate to adjust your settings if you find that another configuration suits you better over time.

6. Advanced Tips for Professionals

For experienced photographers, fine-tuning the EOS R50's button functions can enhance efficiency even further:

- **Use Back-Button Focus**: This separates focusing from shutter release, helpful in dynamic settings where you need to lock focus without immediately capturing an image. Professionals may prefer this method for subjects that move unpredictably.

- **Quick Access to Exposure Lock**: Assigning a button to **AE Lock** can be beneficial for scenes with high contrast. This lets you lock exposure before reframing, ensuring consistent brightness across multiple shots.

- **Fast Drive Mode Switching**: Assign the **M-Fn** button to drive mode to switch between single and burst shooting modes instantly. This is ideal for fast-paced situations where you might switch between photographing a single subject and capturing action.

Conclusion

By tailoring the function buttons and shortcuts on your Canon EOS R50, you can build a more intuitive shooting experience that's fully suited to your needs. Whether you're adjusting ISO on the fly, setting up back-button focus, or using the touchscreen shortcuts for quick control, customizing your camera helps you take photos without disruption. Beginners may want to start with a few key customizations, while professionals can fully configure the camera to match their specific workflow. With these settings, you'll have instant access to the controls you use most, making the Canon EOS R50 an even more powerful tool in your hands.

CHAPTER 4

UNDERSTANDING EXPOSURE AND FOCUS

Exposure Basics: Aperture, Shutter Speed, ISO

Exposure is at the heart of every photograph. It determines how bright or dark an image appears, which directly impacts the mood and detail captured in a scene. Getting the right exposure is particularly important for users of the Canon EOS R50, whether you're a beginner wanting crisp, well-lit shots or a professional looking to fine-tune your creative expression.

Exposure is controlled by three primary settings: **Aperture**, **Shutter Speed**, and **ISO**. These settings, often referred to as the "Exposure Triangle," work together to control the amount of light that reaches the camera sensor. By understanding and mastering each of these components, you'll be able to achieve consistent, high-quality shots in various lighting conditions.

Let's dive into each component:

Aperture: Controlling the Depth and Amount of Light

Aperture is the opening in the lens through which light enters the camera. Think of it as the "pupil" of the camera; a wider aperture allows more light to enter, while a narrower aperture restricts the light. The aperture size is measured in f-stops, such as f/1.8, f/4, f/8, and f/16. The f-number might seem confusing initially because smaller numbers (like f/1.8) actually mean a **larger** aperture, while larger numbers (like f/16) mean a **smaller** aperture.

1. **How Aperture Affects Light**:
    - The wider the aperture (lower f-stop), the more light that reaches the sensor. This is useful in low-light situations, such as indoor settings or nighttime photography, where more light is needed for a properly exposed image.
    - A narrow aperture (higher f-stop) lets in less light, which can be beneficial in bright environments to avoid overexposure. For example, shooting outdoors in direct sunlight often requires a narrower aperture to keep the image from appearing too bright.

2. **Aperture and Depth of Field**:
    - Aperture also controls **depth of field**, which is the zone of the image that appears in sharp focus. A wider aperture (f/1.8) results in a shallow depth of field, making the subject stand out against a blurred background, ideal for portrait photography. This effect is often sought after to create that beautiful background "bokeh" (blurred effect).

- Conversely, a narrower aperture (f/8 or higher) increases the depth of field, meaning more of the image will be in focus. This is useful in landscape photography, where you want both the foreground and background to be sharp and clear.

3. **Adjusting Aperture on the Canon EOS R50**:
    - To adjust the aperture on your Canon EOS R50, switch to **Aperture Priority Mode (Av)**. In this mode, you set the desired f-stop, and the camera automatically adjusts the shutter speed to achieve a balanced exposure.
    - Alternatively, in **Manual Mode (M)**, you can set both the aperture and shutter speed yourself. Experiment with different f-stops to see how it affects both lighting and depth of field.

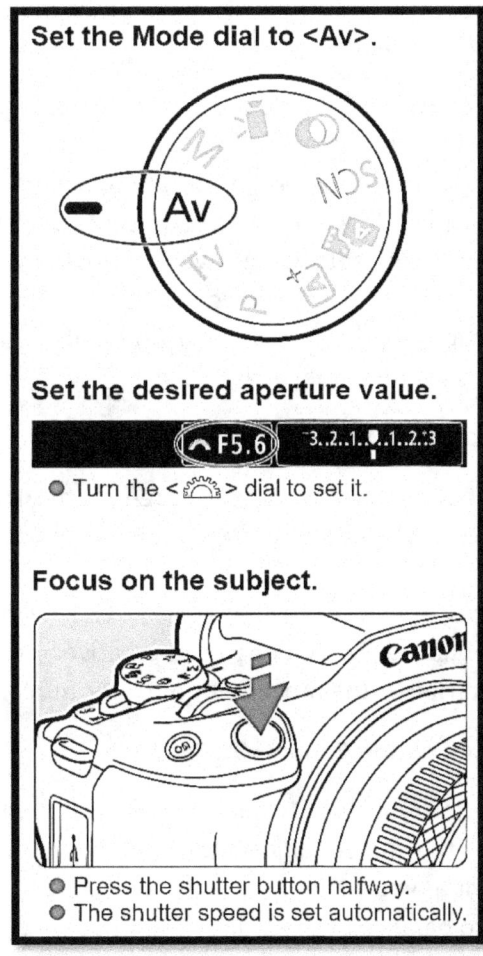

> **Check the display and shoot.**
>
>
>
> - As long as the shutter speed is not blinking, the standard exposure will be obtained.

Shutter Speed: Freezing or Blurring Motion

Shutter speed refers to how long the camera's sensor is exposed to light. It's essentially the "blink" of the camera's eye. The longer the shutter remains open, the more light reaches the sensor. Shutter speed is measured in fractions of a second, such as 1/500, 1/60, 1/2, or even longer in full seconds.

1. **How Shutter Speed Affects Light:**

    - A **fast shutter speed** (e.g., 1/1000 of a second) lets in less light because the sensor is exposed for a shorter time. This is useful in bright conditions or when you want to freeze fast motion, like a bird in flight or a moving car.
    - A **slow shutter speed** (e.g., 1/10 of a second or slower) allows more light in, which is helpful in low-light settings. However, slower shutter speeds can result in motion blur if the camera or subject moves. This can be an intentional creative choice (e.g., capturing light trails or a sense of motion) or something to avoid when aiming for a sharp image.

2. **Shutter Speed and Motion:**

    - With a fast shutter speed, you can "freeze" motion. This is crucial in sports photography or any situation where you want to capture a moving subject with sharp detail.
    - A slower shutter speed introduces motion blur, where moving elements in the scene appear blurred. This can be used creatively, such as capturing the flow of water in a waterfall or the movement of traffic at night.

3. **Adjusting Shutter Speed on the Canon EOS R50:**

    - Use **Shutter Priority Mode (Tv)** on the Canon EOS R50 to set the shutter speed manually while the camera adjusts the aperture to maintain balanced exposure.
    - In **Manual Mode**, you have full control over both shutter speed and aperture, allowing you to balance both settings to suit your scene.

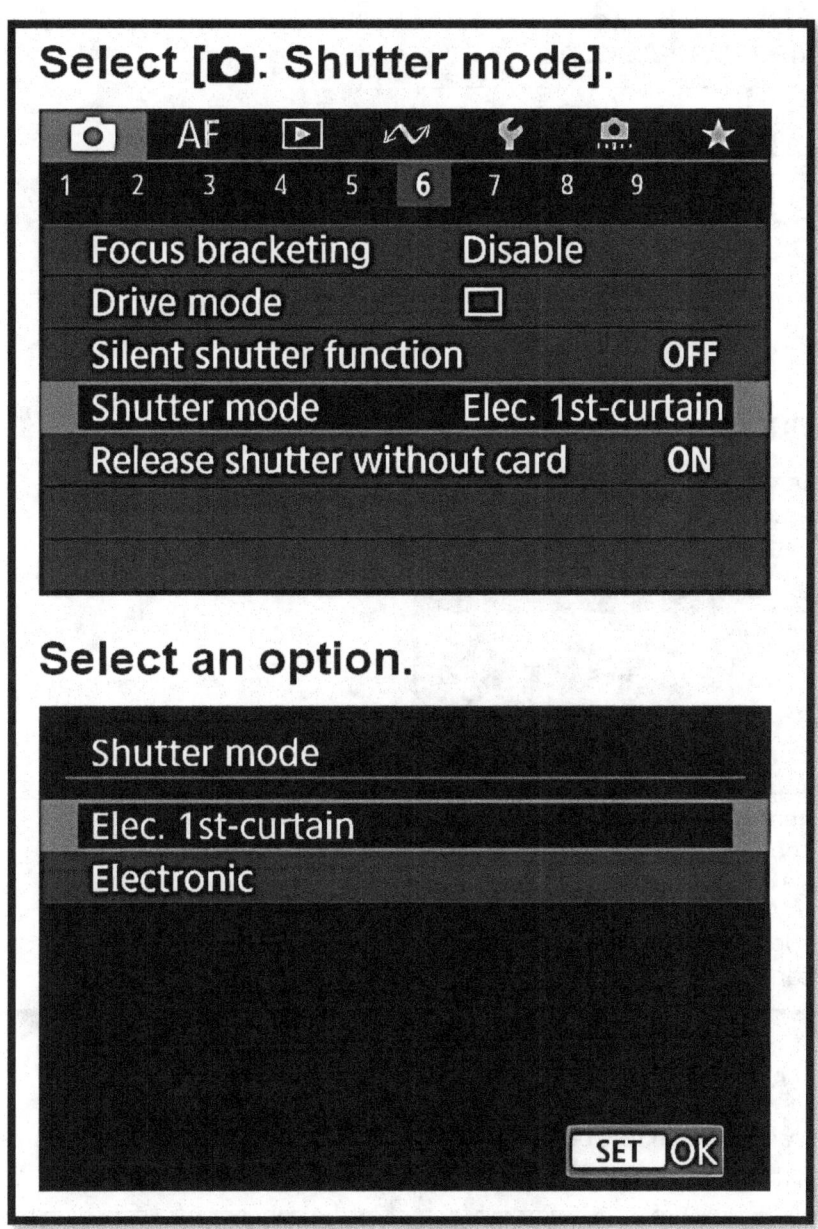

ISO: Adjusting Sensitivity to Light

ISO is the camera's sensitivity to light. A low ISO value means the sensor is less sensitive to light, which is ideal for brightly lit environments. A higher ISO increases sensitivity, making the camera more responsive to low light. On the Canon EOS R50, ISO ranges typically from 100 to higher values, like 25600 or beyond.

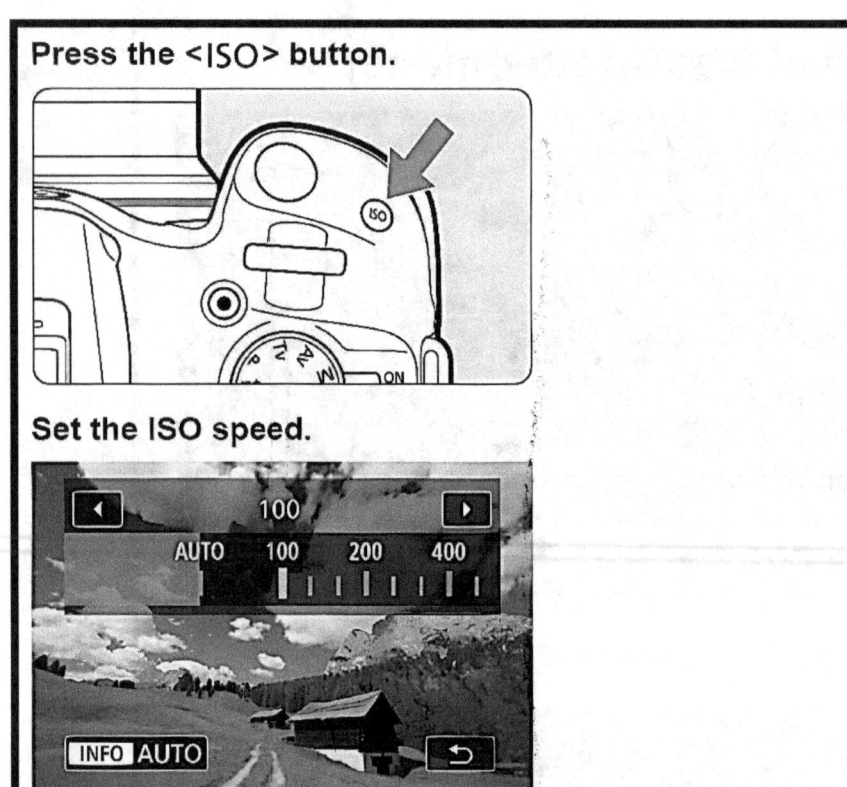

- Turn the <⚙> dial to set it.
- ISO speed can be set within ISO 100–32000 in 1/3-stop increments.
- With [**AUTO**] selected, ISO speed is set automatically.
- When [**AUTO**] is selected, pressing the shutter button halfway will display the ISO speed actually set.
- You can also press the <INFO> button to set the speed to [**AUTO**].

1. **How ISO Affects Light and Noise:**

    - A **low ISO** (e.g., 100 or 200) produces the cleanest images with the least noise, which is ideal for daylight photography or well-lit scenes.
    - A **high ISO** (e.g., 1600 or more) makes the sensor more sensitive to light, allowing you to shoot in darker conditions without adjusting aperture or shutter speed. However, higher ISO settings often introduce noise, or graininess, in the image, which can reduce sharpness and clarity.

2. **When to Adjust ISO:**

    - Use a low ISO in bright lighting conditions to maintain the highest image quality.

- Increase the ISO when shooting indoors or in dim lighting to avoid using very slow shutter speeds, which might result in motion blur, or very wide apertures, which may not suit every situation.
- When using a higher ISO on the Canon EOS R50, you can also apply noise reduction either in-camera or during post-processing to improve image quality.

3. **Adjusting ISO on the Canon EOS R50**:
   - The Canon EOS R50 allows you to set ISO manually or use **Auto ISO**. In Auto ISO, the camera chooses the ISO based on the lighting conditions, which is convenient for quick shots.
   - In **Manual Mode**, you can set the ISO along with aperture and shutter speed, giving you full control over all aspects of exposure.

Balancing Aperture, Shutter Speed, and ISO: The Exposure Triangle

Understanding the relationship between aperture, shutter speed, and ISO is essential for mastering exposure. Here's a summary of how these elements interact:

- **Aperture** affects the amount of light entering the lens and controls depth of field.
- **Shutter Speed** determines how long the sensor is exposed to light and can freeze or blur motion.
- **ISO** adjusts the camera's sensitivity to light, impacting noise levels in your images.

For example, in a low-light environment, you might need to widen the aperture to let in more light, slow down the shutter speed to avoid underexposure, or raise the ISO to avoid motion blur or shallow depth of field.

Practical Tips for Canon EOS R50 Users

1. **Practice with Aperture Priority (Av) and Shutter Priority (Tv) Modes**:

   Experimenting with Av and Tv modes is an effective way to get comfortable with adjusting exposure without worrying about all three settings at once.

2. **Use the Exposure Compensation Feature**:

   When shooting in Av or Tv mode, you can also use exposure compensation to fine-tune brightness. This is especially useful in challenging lighting situations, like high-contrast scenes.

3. **Experiment with Different Lighting Conditions**:

Try shooting at different times of the day or indoors with varying light sources to observe how each exposure setting impacts the result.

Conclusion

Mastering aperture, shutter speed, and ISO on the Canon EOS R50 allows you to create images with the exact look and feel you envision, whether you're capturing a dimly lit interior or a bright, sunny landscape.

Autofocus Modes and Area Selection

Mastering autofocus (AF) is crucial in photography, as it determines how your subject appears in the final image—whether it's tack sharp or slightly blurred. The Canon EOS R50 offers a powerful autofocus system designed for both beginners and professionals, with features to help capture sharp images in various shooting conditions.

The camera's autofocus system includes multiple modes and area selection options, allowing you to adjust how and where the camera focuses. Each mode and area selection option serves a unique purpose, so understanding when to use them can significantly improve your photography.

Autofocus Modes on the Canon EOS R50

The Canon EOS R50 has different autofocus modes that control how the camera continuously or briefly focuses on a subject. These modes are particularly useful depending on whether your subject is stationary, moving, or unpredictably changing positions. Here's a breakdown of the primary autofocus modes:

1. **One-Shot AF (Single Autofocus)**:
    - **What it is**: One-Shot AF is designed for still subjects. In this mode, the camera focuses on your subject when you press the shutter button halfway. Once the focus is locked, it won't adjust further until you release the shutter button and press it again.
    - **When to use it**: This mode is best for static subjects, like portraits, landscapes, or still-life photography, where the subject's position doesn't change. It ensures a sharp focus on a single point without the need for continuous refocusing.
    - **How to use it**: Point the camera at your subject and press the shutter button halfway. The camera will lock focus, and you can then press the shutter fully to capture the image. If your subject moves, however, you'll need to refocus.

2. **AI Servo AF (Continuous Autofocus)**:

- **What it is**: AI Servo AF is ideal for moving subjects. In this mode, the camera continuously adjusts focus as long as you keep the shutter button pressed halfway. The camera "tracks" the subject's movement, making adjustments to keep it in focus.
- **When to use it**: Use AI Servo AF when photographing moving subjects, such as sports, wildlife, or any scene with motion. This mode is designed to help you capture sharp images even if the subject is constantly shifting.
- **How to use it**: Press the shutter button halfway to engage AI Servo AF, and keep it held down as you track the moving subject. The camera will continuously update focus to maintain sharpness on the subject.

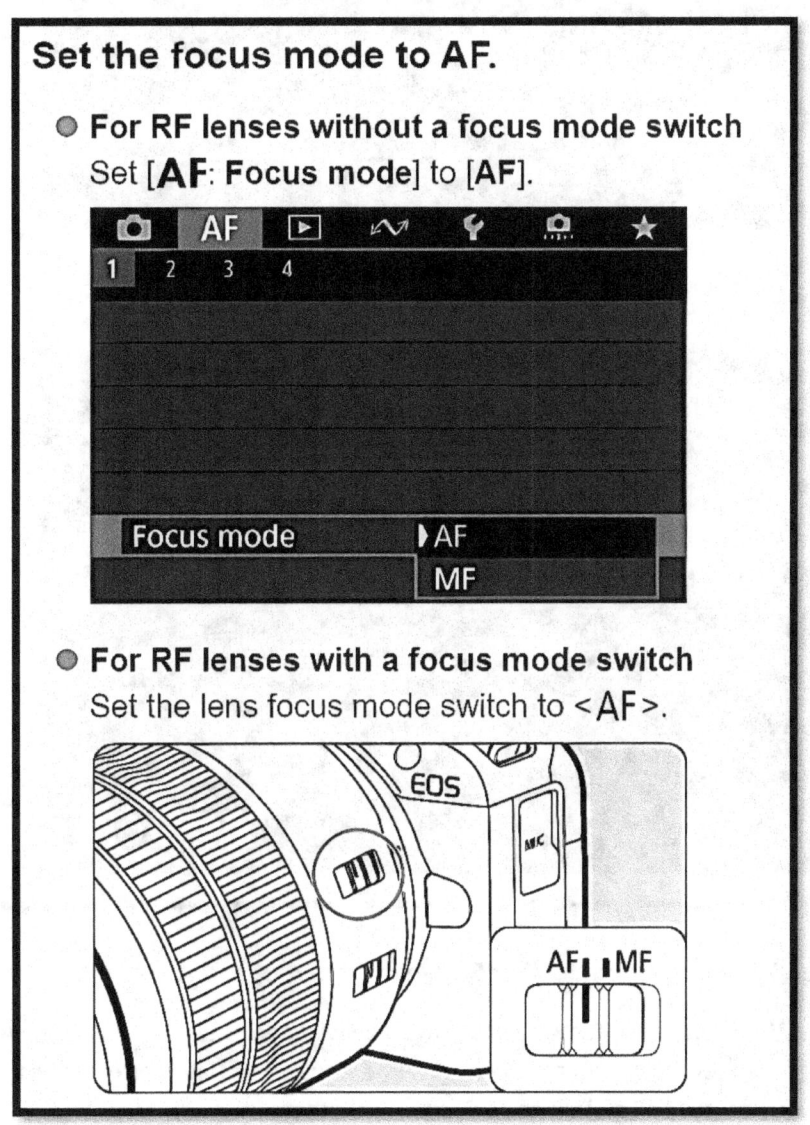

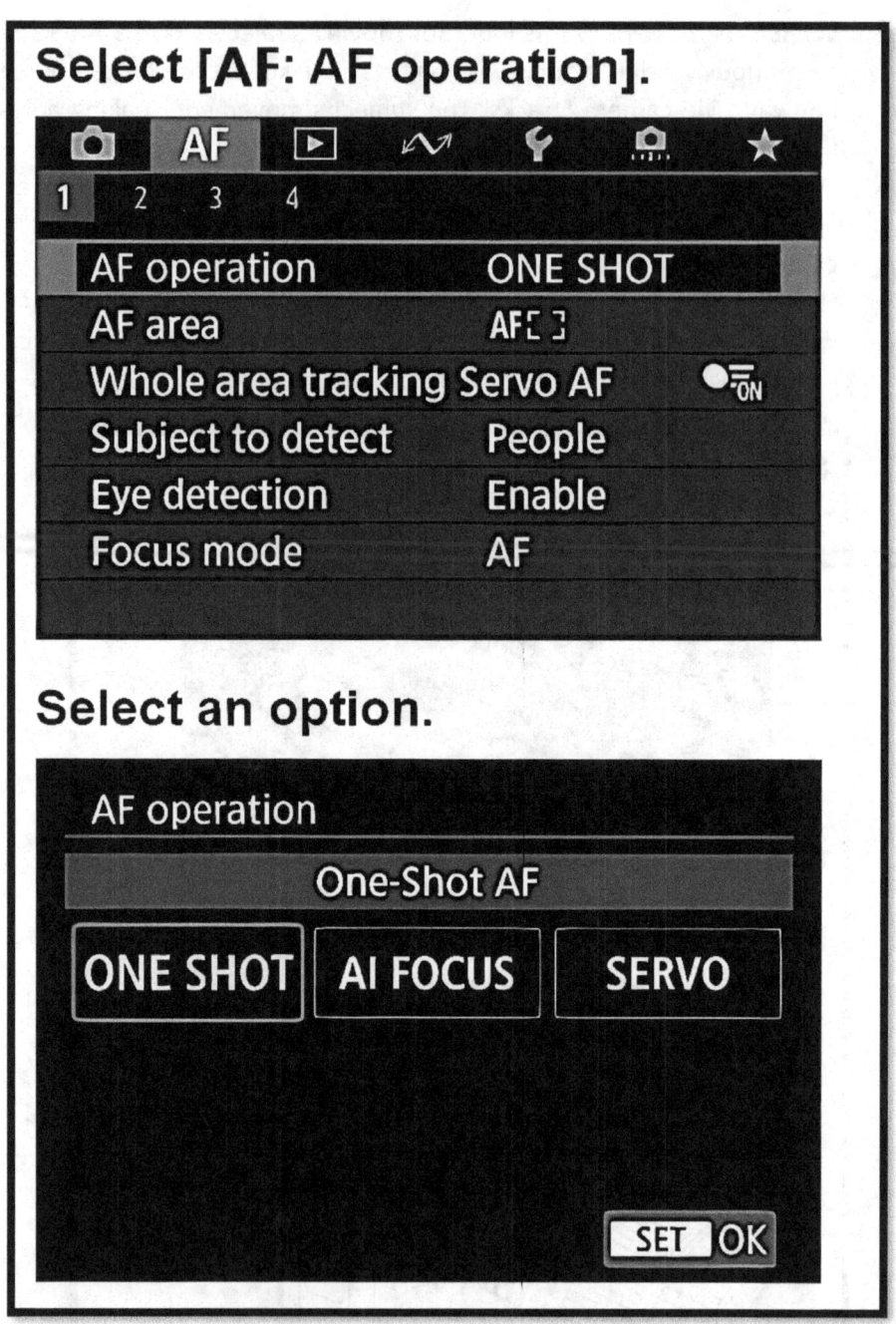

3. **AI Focus AF (Automatic Selection Between One-Shot and AI Servo):**
    - **What it is**: AI Focus AF automatically switches between One-Shot AF and AI Servo AF based on subject movement. The camera initially locks focus like in One-Shot mode but will switch to AI Servo if it detects movement.

- **When to use it**: AI Focus is helpful when you're unsure if your subject will move. It's a versatile option that lets the camera decide whether to maintain a fixed focus or continuously adjust it.
- **How to use it**: Set the camera to AI Focus AF and press the shutter button halfway. The camera will lock focus if the subject is still but will track the subject's movement if it detects any, allowing you to capture both stationary and moving subjects seamlessly.

AF Area Selection Options on the Canon EOS R50

The Canon EOS R50 also allows you to select specific AF areas, meaning you can control where within the frame the camera should focus. This customization helps achieve the desired focus on various subjects, whether they're centered, off-center, or occupy a broad area.

1. **Spot AF**:
    - **What it is**: Spot AF allows you to select a very small and precise focus point within the frame. This mode is ideal for pinpoint accuracy.
    - **When to use it**: Use Spot AF when you need to focus on a specific part of a subject, such as the eye in a portrait or a small detail in a macro shot. It's helpful when you want to focus on a tiny, distinct area without interference from the surroundings.
    - **How to use it**: Select Spot AF in the AF area selection menu, then use the joystick or touchscreen to position the focus point on your subject. This provides you with complete control over where the camera focuses.

2. **1-Point AF**:
    - **What it is**: 1-Point AF uses a single AF point within the frame. This setting is slightly larger than Spot AF, making it useful for focusing on subjects that are still fairly small but need a bit more focus area.
    - **When to use it**: 1-Point AF is ideal for portraits, close-ups, and scenarios where the subject isn't moving but occupies a small area of the frame. It's an excellent balance between precision and ease of use.
    - **How to use it**: Select 1-Point AF in the AF menu and move the focus point to your desired location using the touchscreen or control dial. The camera will then lock focus on the selected area.

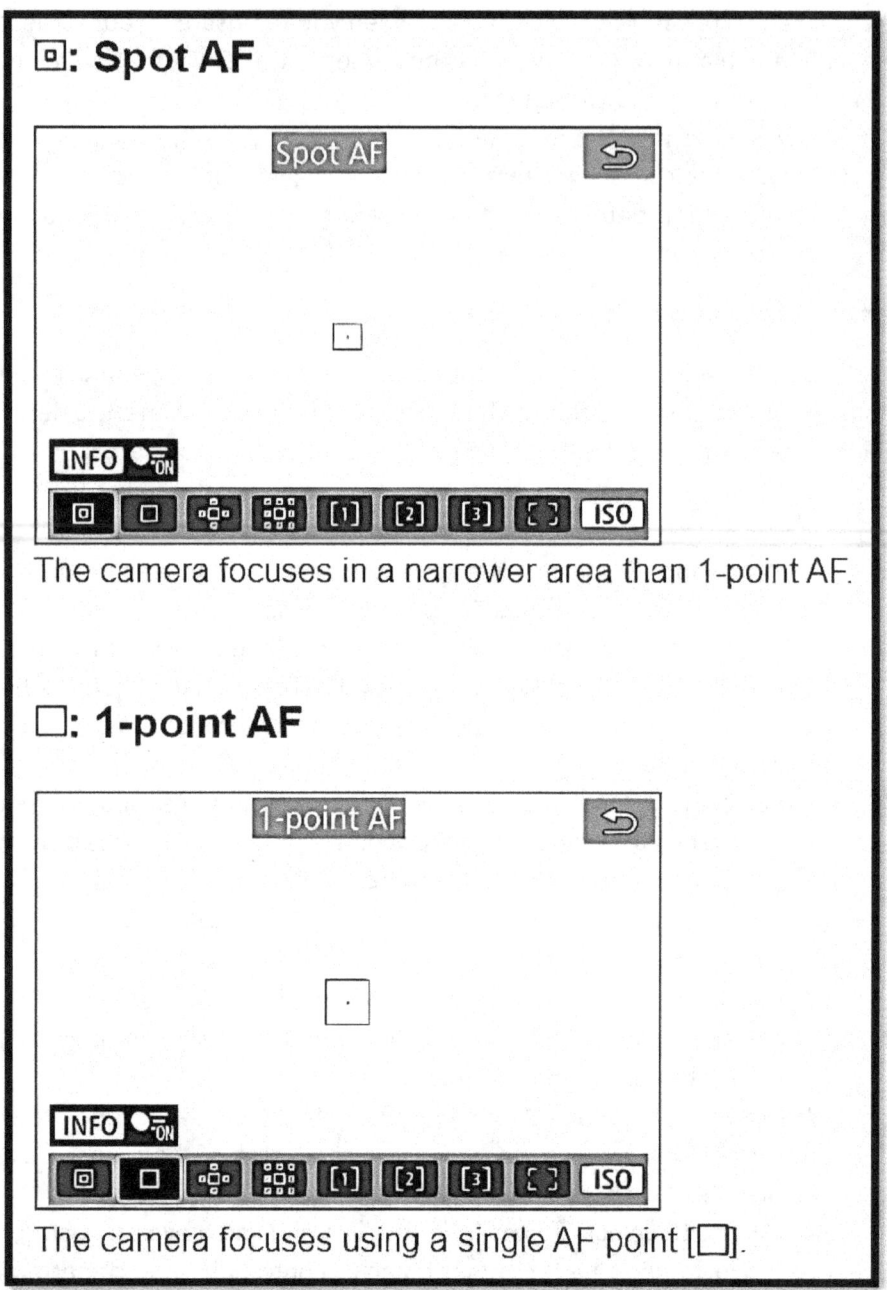

3. **Expand AF Area**:
   - **What it is**: In this mode, the camera uses a primary focus point along with surrounding points to expand the focusing area. If the subject moves slightly away from the main focus point, the surrounding points help maintain focus.

- **When to use it**: Expand AF Area is useful for subjects with limited movement within a small area, such as a child playing or a pet moving around in a restricted space. It provides more flexibility than 1-Point AF.
- **How to use it**: Select Expand AF Area, and choose your main focus point. The camera will then engage the surrounding points to help keep the subject in focus if it moves slightly.

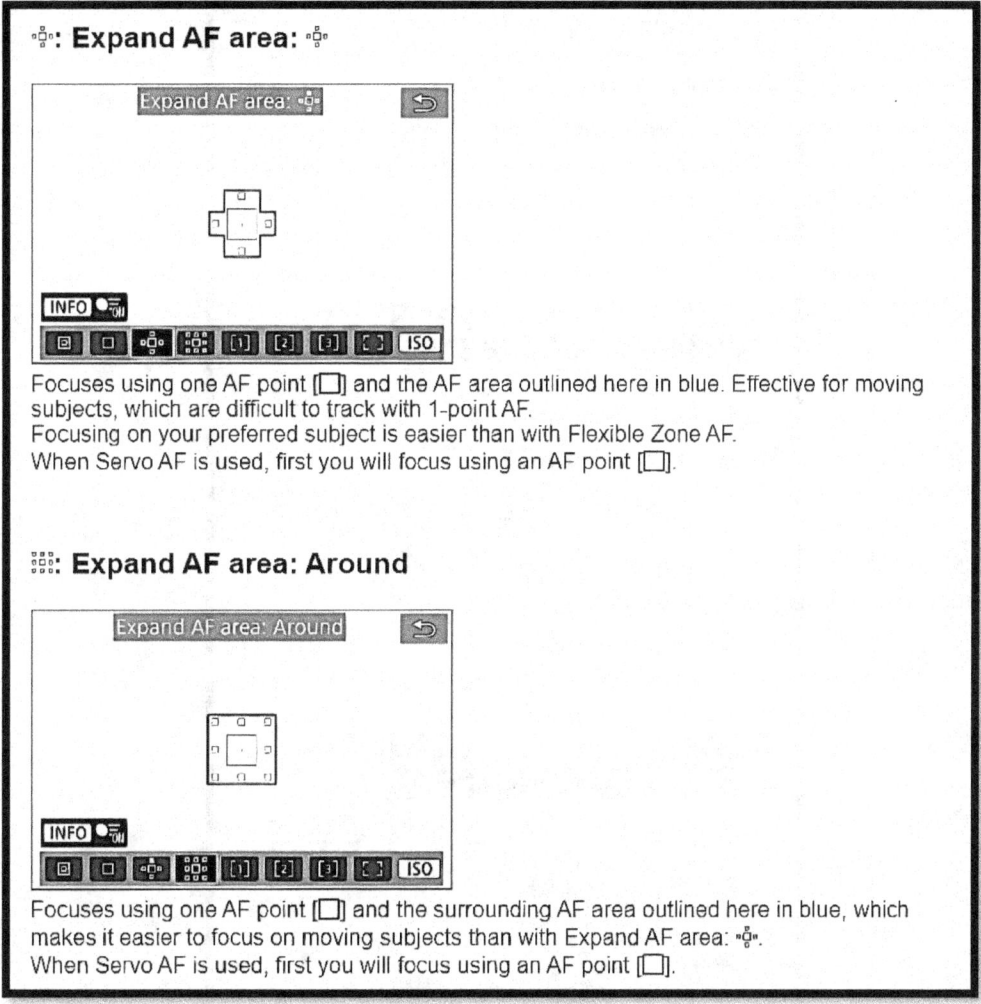

4. **Zone AF**:
    - **What it is**: Zone AF divides the frame into a larger zone, allowing the camera to select a focus point within the chosen area. This gives you control over a general region instead of a specific point.

- **When to use it**: Zone AF works well for subjects that move unpredictably within a certain area, such as a person walking or a pet playing. It provides a wider range for the camera to lock focus within the designated zone.
- **How to use it**: Choose Zone AF in the AF area menu, then select the area of the frame where you want the camera to focus. The camera will prioritize subjects within the chosen zone, maintaining focus even if they move around slightly.

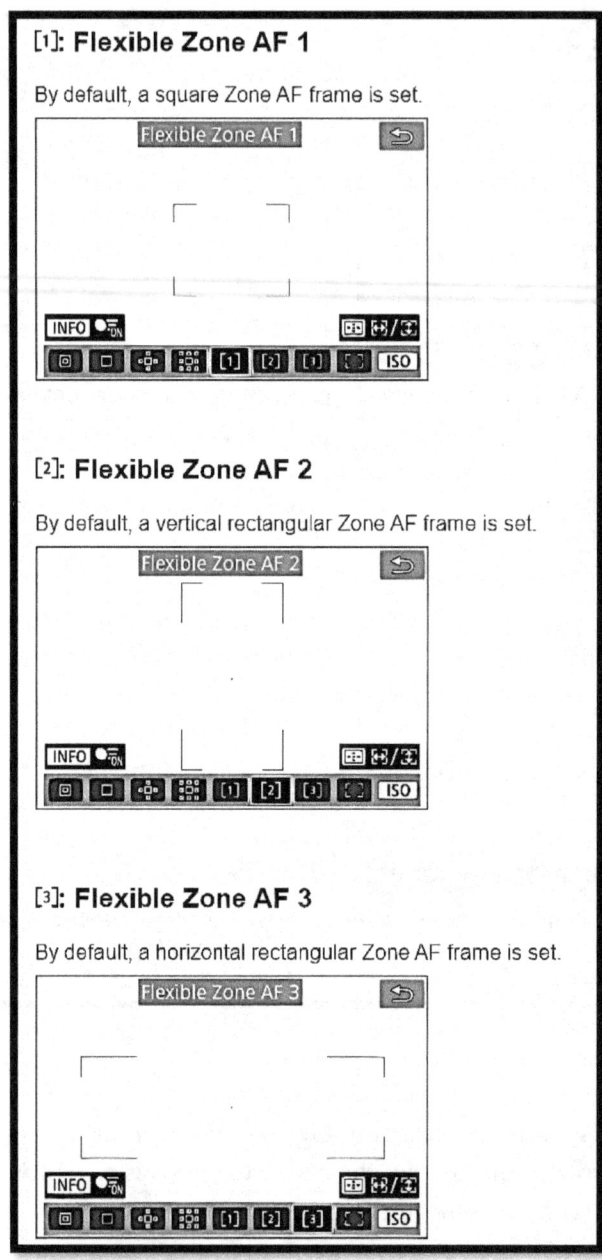

5. **Tracking AF**:
    - **What it is**: Tracking AF (also known as Face and Eye Detection or Object Tracking) detects and follows a subject's face, eyes, or even entire bodies automatically. On the Canon EOS R50, this mode is enhanced by its subject detection capabilities, making it ideal for tracking people, animals, or vehicles.
    - **When to use it**: Use Tracking AF for portraits, action shots, or scenes where you want the camera to automatically adjust focus as the subject moves. It's especially useful in dynamic environments like events, sports, or wildlife photography.
    - **How to use it**: Select Tracking AF, and the camera will detect and lock onto faces, eyes, or moving objects within the frame. You can override the automatic selection by manually choosing an initial point, which the camera will track.

Combining Autofocus Modes and AF Areas for Different Scenarios

Understanding how to combine autofocus modes and AF areas is essential for capturing various types of photography effectively. Here's a quick guide to using these features together:

1. **For Portraits**:

    Use **One-Shot AF** with **1-Point AF** or **Spot AF** to lock focus precisely on the subject's eyes. If the subject might move slightly, consider **Tracking AF** for face and eye detection.

2. **For Landscapes**:

    Use **One-Shot AF** with a **wide AF area** or **Zone AF** to focus on a broad section of the scene. This allows you to capture a deep depth of field while ensuring clarity throughout the landscape.

3. **For Sports or Action Photography**:

    Set the camera to **AI Servo AF** with **Tracking AF** or **Expand AF Area**. This combination allows the camera to continuously adjust focus as your subject moves rapidly across the frame.

4. **For Wildlife Photography**:

    Choose **AI Servo AF** with **Zone AF** or **Tracking AF** for animal face and eye detection. This setting helps you maintain sharp focus on animals moving unpredictably, particularly when tracking birds or mammals.

5. **For Macro Photography**:

Select **One-Shot AF** with **Spot AF** for precise focusing on tiny details. This will allow you to zero in on small subjects, like insects or flowers, where even slight focus shifts can affect the final image.

Conclusion

By mastering the autofocus modes and area selections on your Canon EOS R50, you gain control over how and where your camera focuses, allowing for sharper, more compelling images. Whether you're capturing a quick candid shot, following fast-moving subjects, or crafting precise macro photography, these autofocus settings give you the flexibility to adapt to any shooting scenario confidently.

Metering Modes and Exposure Compensation

Accurate exposure is essential to capturing well-balanced photographs, as it ensures that your image is neither too dark nor too bright. Exposure is controlled by three main settings: aperture, shutter speed, and ISO, but understanding how your camera reads light is just as important. This is where metering modes and exposure compensation come into play. These features allow you to control how the Canon EOS R50 evaluates light in a scene and adjust the exposure as needed to capture images that look exactly as you want.

In this section, we'll explore metering modes and exposure compensation in detail, helping both beginners and professionals understand how to make the most of these tools.

Metering Modes on the Canon EOS R50

Metering modes help your Canon EOS R50 analyze the light in a scene and determine the best exposure settings for a balanced image. The camera uses its built-in light meter to evaluate brightness levels, but different metering modes allow you to control how the camera prioritizes certain areas of the frame when measuring light.

Types of Metering Modes

The Canon EOS R50 offers several metering modes, each tailored to different shooting situations:

1. **Evaluative Metering**:
    - **What it is**: Evaluative metering (also known as matrix metering in other brands) is the most commonly used metering mode on the Canon EOS R50. This mode divides the entire frame into multiple zones and analyzes light levels across all of them. The camera then considers the entire scene to determine the exposure.
    - **When to use it**: Evaluative metering is ideal for most general photography situations, especially when the lighting is balanced or if you're unsure of which metering mode to use. It works well for landscapes, portraits, and even action shots where the lighting is not overly complicated.

- **How to use it**: Set your camera to Evaluative metering in the menu, and the camera will automatically analyze light across the frame. You don't need to adjust much; the camera does most of the work for you. However, if you notice that the subject looks too dark or too bright, you may need to use exposure compensation to make adjustments (more on this below).

2. **Partial Metering**:
    - **What it is**: Partial metering evaluates the light within a smaller area in the center of the frame—usually around 6-10% of the image. This mode is useful when you want to meter for a specific area without being influenced by the lighting in the background.
    - **When to use it**: Use Partial metering when your subject is backlit or if the scene has high contrast, such as a person in front of a bright window. This mode helps prioritize the subject in the center, ensuring it's properly exposed even if the background is much brighter.
    - **How to use it**: Select Partial metering from the metering options in your camera menu. Frame your subject so it's positioned in the center of the image, then adjust your exposure based on the light levels within that central area. If needed, reposition your camera or use exposure compensation to fine-tune the results.

3. **Spot Metering**:
    - **What it is**: Spot metering is the most precise metering mode, measuring light from an extremely small area—usually about 2-3% of the frame. It focuses exclusively on a single point, typically the area where your autofocus point is located.
    - **When to use it**: Spot metering is best for situations with extreme contrast, such as photographing a bright subject against a dark background, or when you need accurate exposure on a very specific part of the scene. It's useful for wildlife, macro photography, or any instance where precise exposure control is needed.
    - **How to use it**: Choose Spot metering in the menu, then align your autofocus point with the specific area you want to meter. The camera will adjust exposure based solely on that small spot, ignoring other parts of the scene. Use exposure compensation if the subject still appears over- or underexposed.

4. **Center-Weighted Average Metering**:
    - **What it is**: Center-weighted average metering evaluates the entire frame but places more emphasis on the center. It's a less precise option than spot or partial metering but works well in moderately challenging lighting.

- **When to use it**: Center-weighted average is helpful for portraits and scenes where the subject occupies the center of the frame. It's also useful for balanced exposures in scenes that are not heavily backlit or overly contrasted.
- **How to use it**: Set your camera to Center-weighted average metering, and frame your shot so that the subject is centered. The camera will measure the entire scene, prioritizing the center for exposure calculations.

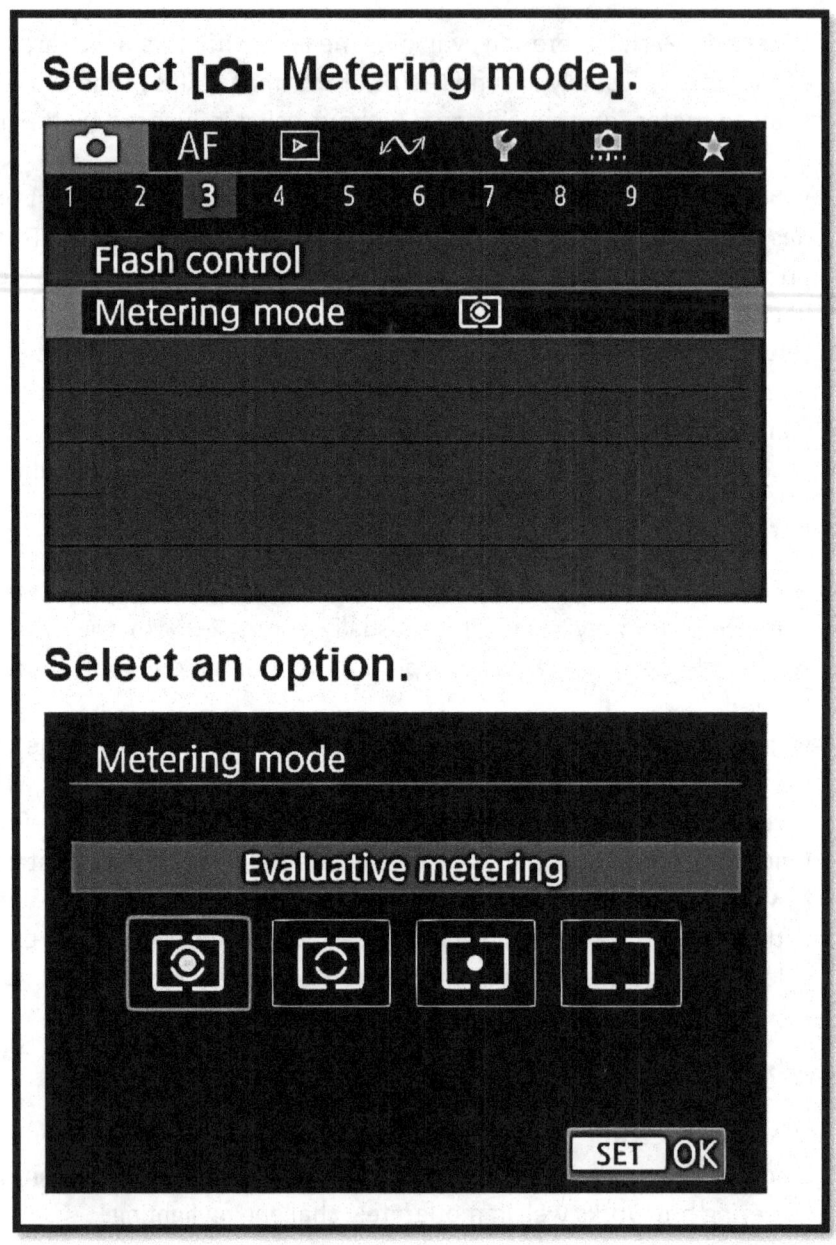

> ⦿: **Evaluative metering**
> General-purpose metering mode suited even for backlit subjects. The camera adjusts the exposure automatically to suit the scene.
>
> ◉: **Partial metering**
> Effective where there are much brighter lights around the subject due to backlight, etc. The partial metering area is indicated on the screen.
>
> [·]: **Spot metering**
> Effective when metering a specific part of the subject. The spot metering area is indicated on the screen.
>
> [ ]: **Center-weighted average**
> The metering across the screen is averaged, with the center of the screen weighted more heavily.

Exposure Compensation on the Canon EOS R50

Even with the right metering mode, your camera might sometimes produce images that are slightly too dark (underexposed) or too bright (overexposed). This can happen in tricky lighting conditions, such as backlighting or scenes with high contrast. Exposure compensation allows you to adjust the exposure manually without changing your metering mode or other settings, giving you more control over the final image.

> **Check the exposure.**
>
> ● Press the shutter button halfway and check the exposure level indicator.
>
> **Set the compensation amount.**
> Increased exposure, to brighten images
>
>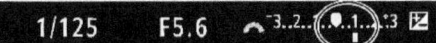
>
> Decreased exposure, to darken images
>
>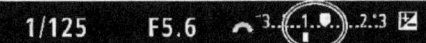
>
> ● To set the amount, press the <▲> key to select exposure compensation and watch the screen as you turn the <🗘> dial.
> ● A [🔆] icon is displayed to indicate exposure compensation.
>
> **Take the picture.**
>
> ● To cancel exposure compensation, set the exposure level [❚] to the standard exposure index ([▼]).

What is Exposure Compensation?

Exposure compensation is a feature that lets you adjust the brightness of an image by altering the exposure settings. On the Canon EOS R50, you can typically adjust exposure compensation by up to ±3 stops, which allows you to make subtle or dramatic changes to the exposure. Each stop represents a doubling or halving of the amount of light entering the camera, allowing for fine adjustments.

When and How to Use Exposure Compensation

Knowing when to use exposure compensation is essential for achieving the right look in your photos. Here are some common situations and tips for using exposure compensation effectively:

1. **Backlit Scenes**:
   - **Challenge**: When photographing a subject against a bright background, such as a person standing in front of a window or the sun, the camera may underexpose the subject because it meters for the bright background.
   - **Solution**: Use exposure compensation to increase the brightness. Set the compensation to +1 or +2 stops to allow more light and properly expose the subject, making it stand out against the bright background.

2. **High-Contrast Situations**:
   - **Challenge**: In scenes with both very dark and very bright areas, like a sunset or a spotlighted subject, the camera might struggle to balance the exposure evenly.
   - **Solution**: Adjust exposure compensation based on your preference. For instance, if you want more detail in the shadows, add positive exposure compensation (+1 or +2). If you want to emphasize the highlights, reduce exposure compensation slightly (-1 or -2).

3. **Snow or Beach Scenes**:
   - **Challenge**: Bright environments like snow or beach scenes can often trick the camera into underexposing the image, making it appear darker than it actually is.
   - **Solution**: Apply positive exposure compensation (around +1 or +1.5) to brighten the image. This will help capture the true brightness of the scene without making it look dull or gray.

4. **Night Photography**:
   - **Challenge**: In low-light or night photography, the camera may overexpose the scene to try to capture details in the darkness, resulting in a washed-out effect.

- **Solution**: Apply negative exposure compensation (-1 or -2) to maintain the dark, atmospheric look of the night scene. This will help preserve highlights like city lights or stars.

Tips for Using Metering Modes and Exposure Compensation Together

1. **Select the Right Metering Mode for the Scene**: Start by choosing the metering mode that best matches your subject and lighting conditions. For instance, use Evaluative metering for balanced scenes, Spot metering for high contrast, and Partial metering for backlit subjects.

2. **Use Exposure Compensation to Fine-Tune**: After choosing the metering mode, take a test shot. If the image appears too dark or too bright, use exposure compensation to adjust the brightness. This allows you to keep your metering mode while controlling exposure to get the desired result.

3. **Practice with Different Scenarios**: Experimenting with metering modes and exposure compensation in various lighting conditions will help you learn how to quickly assess what settings work best. Try using different combinations in everyday scenes, like a backlit portrait or a bright landscape, to see how the adjustments affect your images.

4. **Check the Histogram**: The Canon EOS R50 includes a histogram display, which can be a helpful tool for evaluating exposure. If you notice the histogram is heavily skewed to the left (indicating underexposure) or the right (indicating overexposure), consider using exposure compensation to correct it.

Conclusion

Understanding metering modes and exposure compensation on the Canon EOS R50 enables you to capture images with the perfect brightness level in any situation. Whether you're shooting a backlit portrait, a high-contrast scene, or a bright beach, these tools provide the flexibility to adapt to the lighting and capture the shot you envision. With practice, adjusting metering modes and exposure compensation will become second nature, allowing you to handle even the most challenging lighting with confidence.

CHAPTER 5

CREATIVE SHOOTING MODES

Manual, Aperture Priority, Shutter Priority, and Program Modes

The Canon EOS R50 offers multiple shooting modes that allow photographers to control the camera's exposure settings. Each of these modes—Manual, Aperture Priority, Shutter Priority, and Program—provides a unique balance between automation and manual control, which can be useful depending on your skill level, the type of shot you're aiming for, and the conditions in which you're shooting.

In this section, we'll dive into each of these four main shooting modes, explaining how they work, when to use them, and how you can access them on the Canon EOS R50.

Manual Mode (M)

What It Is: Manual mode gives you full control over all exposure settings, including aperture, shutter speed, and ISO. In this mode, the camera does not automatically adjust any settings for you, so you can decide exactly how much light enters the camera and how it affects the final image.

When to Use It: Manual mode is best suited for photographers who want complete control over every aspect of exposure. It's particularly useful in challenging lighting conditions, like night photography or studio photography, where consistent settings are essential. Manual mode is also popular among photographers who prefer a high level of customization or need precise exposure adjustments for creative effects.

How to Use Manual Mode:

- **Setting Aperture**: Use the main control dial on the Canon EOS R50 to adjust the aperture. A lower f-stop (e.g., f/2.8) allows more light and creates a shallow depth of field (blurred background), while a higher f-stop (e.g., f/16) reduces light and increases depth of field (keeping more of the scene in focus).

- **Adjusting Shutter Speed**: Rotate the same dial to set your shutter speed. A slower shutter speed (e.g., 1/30s) captures more light, making it ideal for low-light conditions or creating motion blur. A faster shutter speed (e.g., 1/1000s) reduces the amount of light, useful for freezing fast-moving subjects.

- **Setting ISO**: Navigate to the ISO setting in the camera's menu. A lower ISO (e.g., ISO 100) keeps noise to a minimum, producing clearer images but requires more light. A higher ISO (e.g., ISO 1600) can capture scenes in low light but may introduce graininess.

- **Fine-Tuning Exposure**: After setting the aperture, shutter speed, and ISO, use the camera's exposure meter (visible in the viewfinder or on the screen) to check if your exposure is balanced. Adjust one or more settings as needed until the exposure is close to the center of the meter.

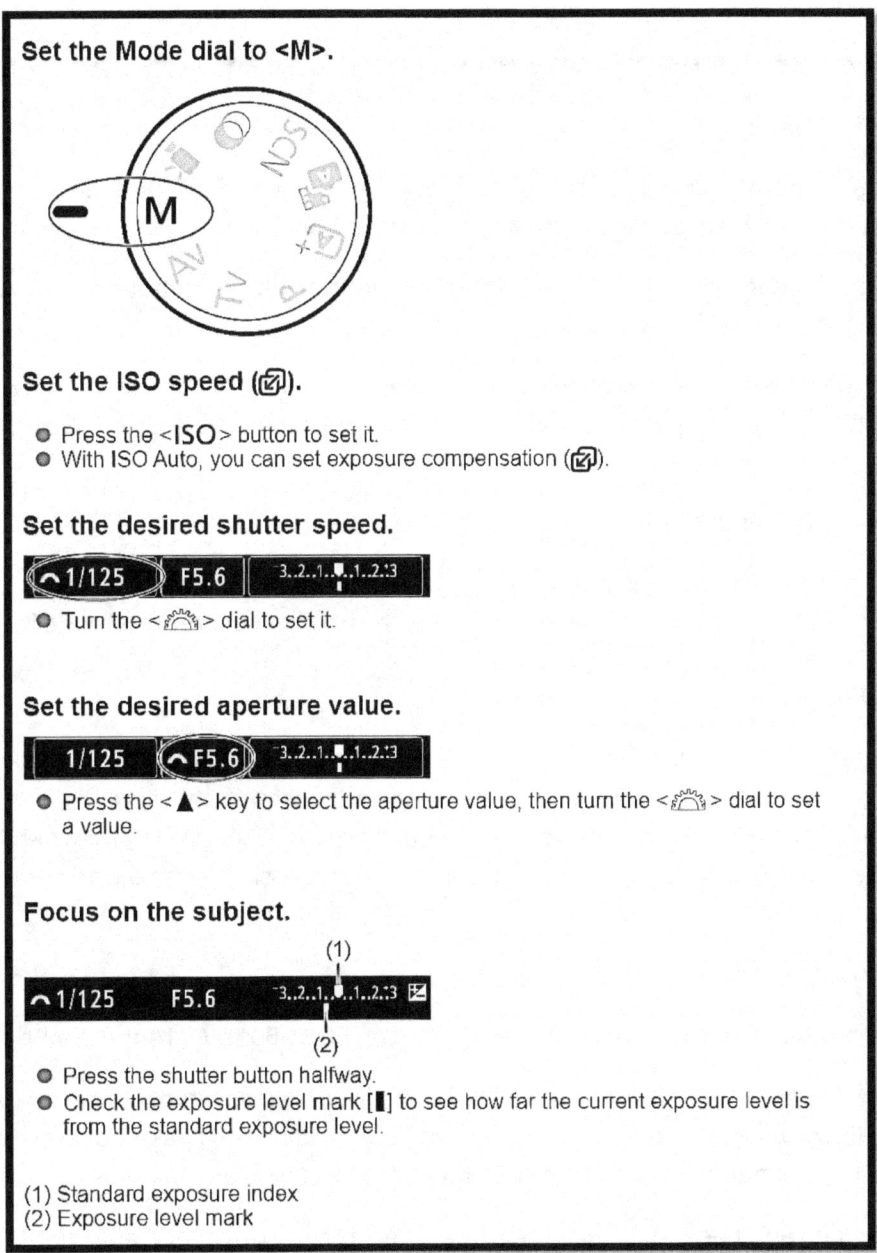

> **Set the exposure and take the picture.**
>
> ⌒ 1/125   F5.6   ⁻3..2..1..●..1..2..3
>
> ○ Check the exposure level indicator and set the desired shutter speed and aperture value.

Tips for Manual Mode:

- **Practice in Static Scenes**: Start with non-moving subjects in a well-lit environment to get familiar with how aperture, shutter speed, and ISO interact.

- **Use a Tripod in Low Light**: Slower shutter speeds can lead to motion blur. A tripod can stabilize the camera, especially in low-light situations.

- **Experiment with Depth of Field and Motion**: Manual mode lets you play with depth of field (by adjusting aperture) and motion blur (by adjusting shutter speed) to achieve various creative effects.

Aperture Priority Mode (Av or A)

What It Is: In Aperture Priority mode, you control the aperture setting while the camera automatically adjusts the shutter speed to achieve a balanced exposure. This mode is useful when you want to control depth of field—how much of the scene is in focus—without worrying about shutter speed adjustments.

When to Use It: Aperture Priority is ideal for portrait photography, where you often want a blurred background to keep focus on your subject, or for landscape photography, where a higher f-stop (smaller aperture) can keep more of the scene in focus. It's also helpful when the lighting is changing frequently, as the camera will automatically adjust shutter speed to maintain proper exposure.

How to Use Aperture Priority Mode:

- **Set the Mode**: Turn the mode dial on the Canon EOS R50 to Av (Aperture Priority).

- **Select Aperture**: Use the control dial to set your desired aperture. Lower f-stop numbers (e.g., f/2.8) will result in a shallow depth of field, making the background appear blurred. Higher f-stop numbers (e.g., f/11) will keep more of the scene in focus.

- **Check Shutter Speed**: Although the camera sets the shutter speed automatically, you can see the chosen shutter speed in the viewfinder or on the screen. If it's too slow (which can lead to blur), consider increasing the ISO to allow a faster shutter speed.

- **Monitor Exposure:** The Canon EOS R50 may let you use exposure compensation in this mode. This can be useful if you want to make the image brighter or darker than what the camera suggests, without changing your aperture.

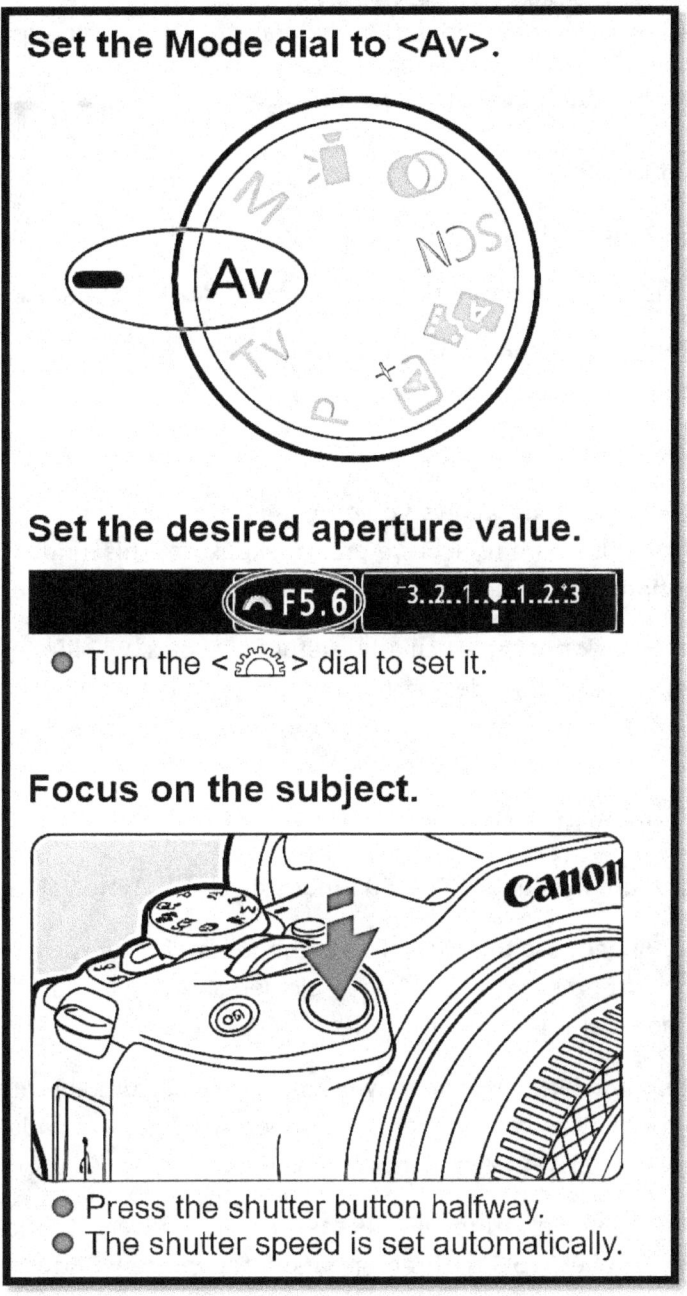

> **Check the display and shoot.**
>
>
>
> - As long as the shutter speed is not blinking, the standard exposure will be obtained.

Tips for Aperture Priority Mode:

- **Portraits**: Use a low f-stop (f/1.8–f/4) for a blurred background.

- **Landscapes**: Use a higher f-stop (f/8–f/16) to keep most of the scene in focus.

- **Low Light**: If you notice the camera is using a slow shutter speed, raise the ISO or use a lens with a wider maximum aperture (low f-stop).

Shutter Priority Mode (Tv or S)

What It Is: Shutter Priority mode allows you to control the shutter speed while the camera automatically adjusts the aperture to achieve proper exposure. This mode is ideal for situations where controlling motion blur or freezing action is more important than depth of field.

When to Use It: Shutter Priority is particularly useful for sports, wildlife, or any type of action photography where you want to freeze fast-moving subjects with a quick shutter speed. It's also helpful for creative motion blur effects, like capturing the flow of water in a river with a slow shutter speed.

How to Use Shutter Priority Mode:

- **Set the Mode**: Turn the Canon EOS R50's mode dial to Tv (Time Value, or Shutter Priority).

- **Select Shutter Speed**: Use the control dial to choose a shutter speed. A fast shutter speed (e.g., 1/1000s) freezes motion, while a slower shutter speed (e.g., 1/30s) captures movement and creates motion blur.

- **Check Aperture and ISO**: The camera will adjust the aperture automatically, but if you're shooting in low light and the camera can't open the aperture wide enough, you might need to increase the ISO to avoid underexposure.

- **Use Exposure Compensation if Necessary**: In Shutter Priority mode, exposure compensation can help you brighten or darken the image without changing the shutter speed, allowing you to retain control over motion effects.

Tips for Shutter Priority Mode:

- **Sports and Action**: Use a shutter speed of at least 1/500s to freeze fast movement.
- **Creative Motion Blur**: For a sense of motion, such as in waterfalls or night-time car lights, use slower shutter speeds like 1/15s or even longer.
- **Check Lighting Conditions**: If the camera cannot balance exposure due to limited aperture, increase the ISO or use a lens with a larger maximum aperture.

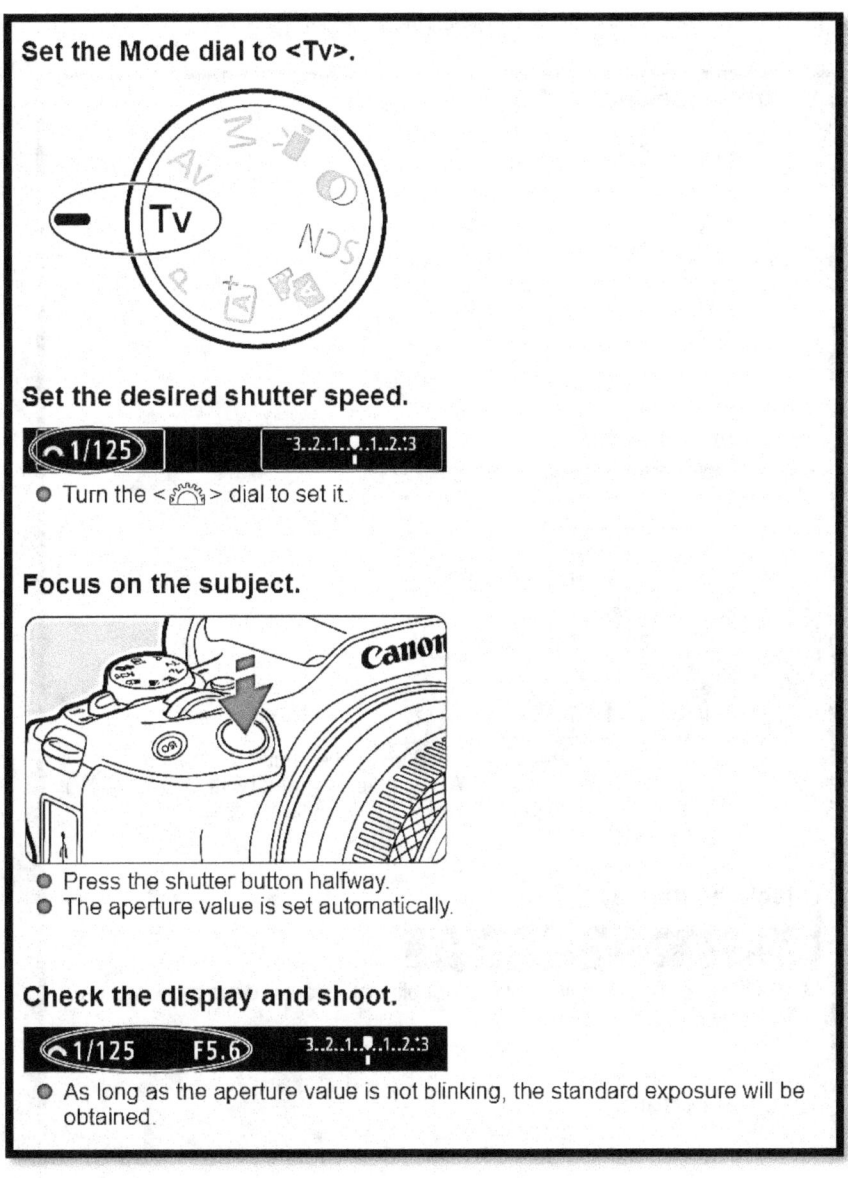

Program Mode (P)

What It Is: Program mode is a semi-automatic mode where the camera chooses both the aperture and shutter speed for balanced exposure, but you can still control certain settings like ISO and exposure compensation. Program mode provides a good balance of convenience and control, making it ideal for quick shots when you don't have time to adjust settings manually.

When to Use It: Program mode is ideal for beginners who want a bit of creative control without the full complexity of Manual mode. It's also great for casual shooting when you want to focus on composition and subject matter rather than technical settings.

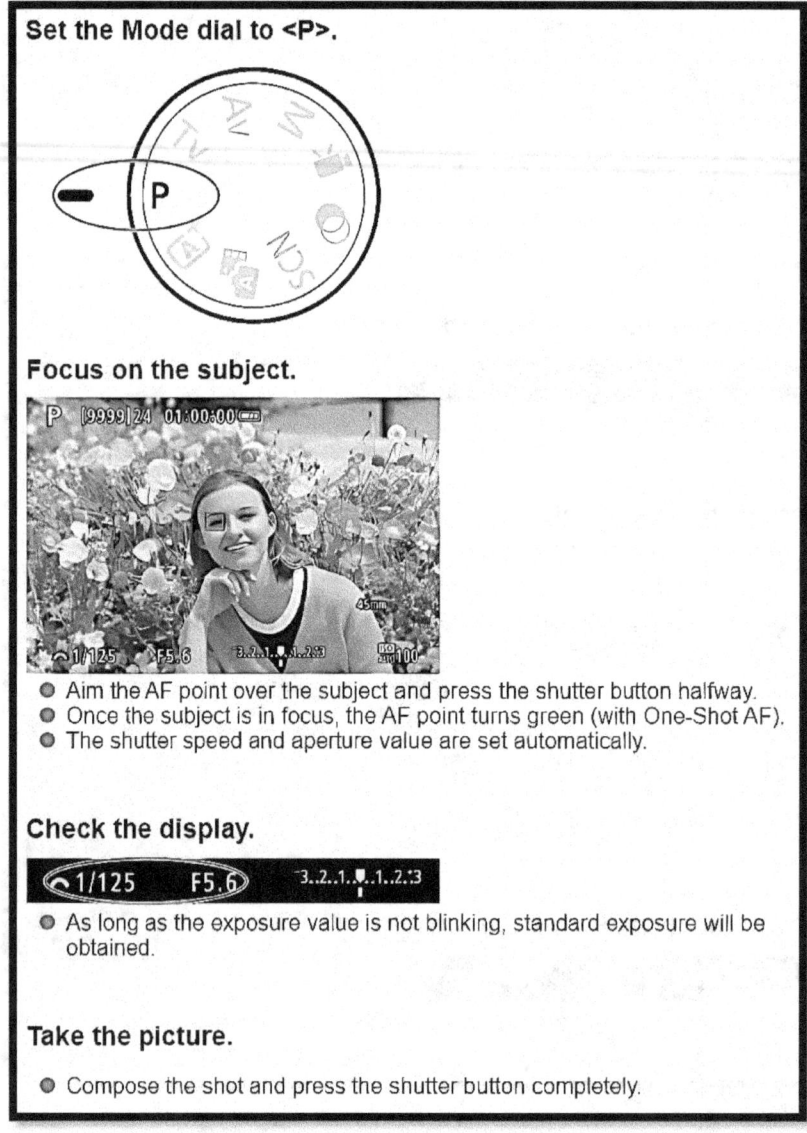

How to Use Program Mode:

- **Set the Mode**: Turn the Canon EOS R50's mode dial to P (Program).

- **Adjust ISO**: You can set the ISO manually, or choose Auto ISO if you want the camera to control all exposure settings. Higher ISO settings will make the camera more sensitive to light, while lower settings keep noise minimal.

- **Use Exposure Compensation**: Program mode allows you to adjust exposure compensation, letting you brighten or darken the image based on the camera's suggested exposure.

- **Experiment with Creative Controls**: Program mode also allows adjustments to other settings like white balance, picture style, and flash control, giving you some flexibility without requiring full manual control.

Tips for Program Mode:

- **Quick and Easy Adjustments**: Program mode is perfect for quick, on-the-go shooting when you need balanced exposure but don't have time to fine-tune settings.

- **Use Exposure Compensation**: If the image appears too bright or too dark, use exposure compensation to adjust the exposure without switching modes.

- **Experiment with Composition**: Since the camera handles exposure, you can focus on framing, angles, and composition.

Conclusion

Each shooting mode on the Canon EOS R50 offers unique advantages and can be used in various situations depending on your needs and comfort level with camera settings. By understanding how each mode functions, you can leverage these options to capture a variety of creative effects, from beautifully blurred backgrounds to action-frozen sports shots, and everything in between. Practicing with each mode will help you develop the skills to quickly adapt to any shooting environment, enhancing your ability to capture well-exposed, professional-looking images.

Scene Modes and Creative Filters

The Canon EOS R50 offers a range of Scene Modes and Creative Filters that simplify the process of capturing specific types of photos while adding creative effects. Scene Modes are designed to optimize camera settings for particular situations, such as capturing portraits, landscapes, or night scenes. Creative Filters allow you to apply artistic effects to your photos directly in-camera, helping you to achieve distinctive looks without needing additional editing software.

In this section, we'll explore the different Scene Modes and Creative Filters available on the Canon EOS R50, explain how each one works, and provide practical tips for making the most of these features.

Scene Modes

Scene Modes are pre-programmed settings that adjust exposure, color, contrast, and other variables based on typical needs for different scenes. These modes are particularly useful for beginners, as they allow you to achieve professional-looking results without needing to understand the full range of camera settings. Let's take a closer look at the most commonly used Scene Modes on the Canon EOS R50.

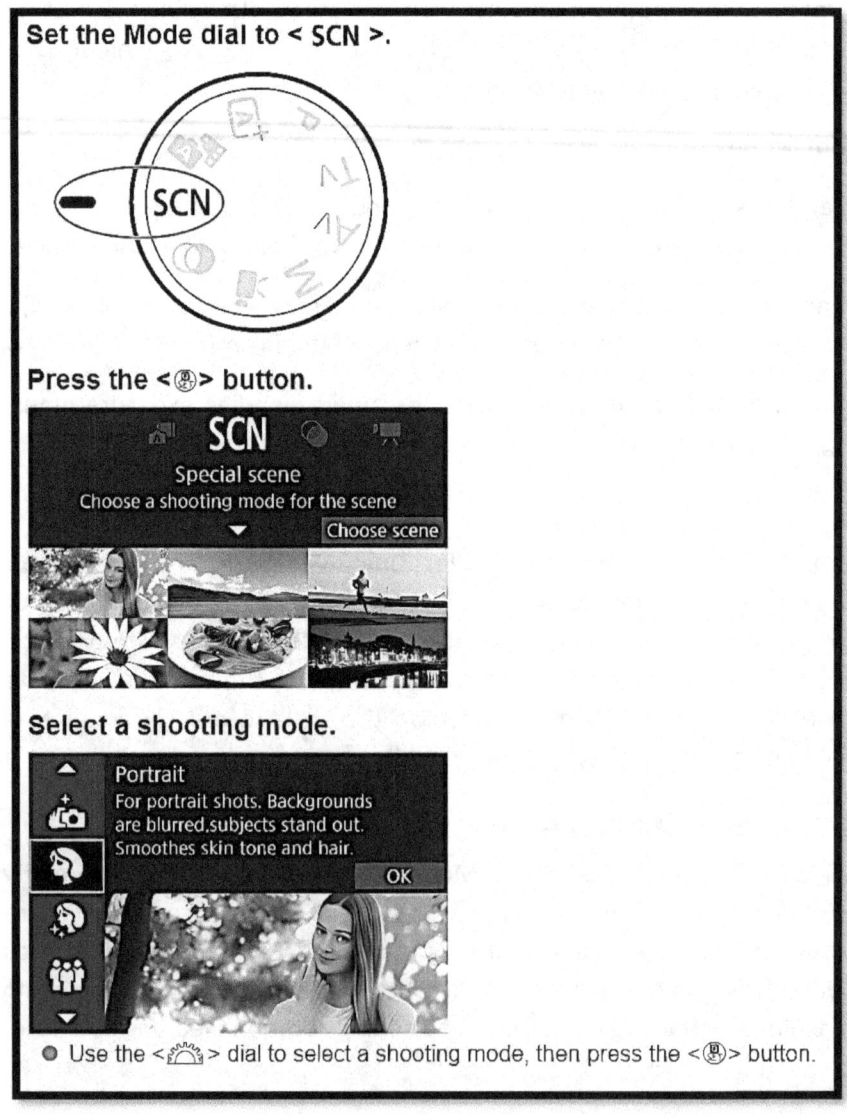

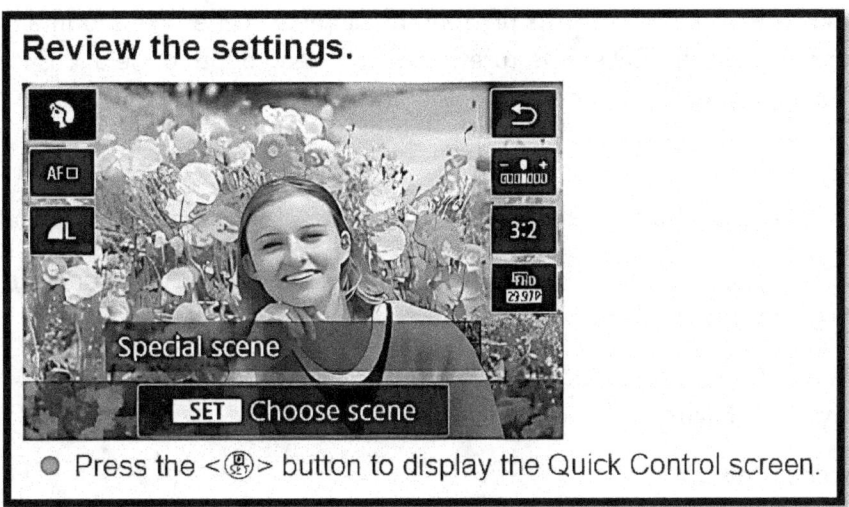

1. Portrait Mode

What It Is: Portrait mode is designed to enhance the appearance of people in your photos. This mode often uses a wider aperture to create a shallow depth of field, which blurs the background and keeps the subject in sharp focus. This helps draw attention to the person you're photographing, making them the focal point of the image.

How It Works:

- The camera automatically sets a wide aperture, reducing depth of field.
- It adjusts the color tone to produce warm, natural skin tones.
- It may also slightly soften the image to give a flattering, smooth look.

Tips for Portrait Mode:

- **Lighting**: Try to use natural light or soft lighting to avoid harsh shadows. If you're outdoors, shoot during the "golden hour" (the hour after sunrise or before sunset) for flattering light.
- **Positioning**: Position your subject a few feet away from the background to increase the blur effect and ensure they stand out.
- **Focus**: Use the camera's eye-detection autofocus if available, as it will help ensure the subject's eyes are sharp, which is crucial for effective portraits.

2. Landscape Mode

What It Is: Landscape mode is ideal for photographing wide scenes like mountains, forests, or cityscapes. This mode sets a smaller aperture to create a deep depth of field, ensuring that most of the scene, from foreground to background, is in focus.

How It Works:

- The camera automatically selects a narrow aperture to increase depth of field.
- It enhances color saturation, especially in blues and greens, to bring out the natural beauty of landscapes.
- The camera may also reduce contrast slightly to prevent details from being lost in shadows or highlights.

Tips for Landscape Mode:

- **Use a Tripod**: A narrow aperture may result in slower shutter speeds, which can cause camera shake. A tripod helps keep the shot stable.
- **Experiment with Angles**: Try capturing the scene from different angles to find the most dynamic composition.
- **Consider HDR Mode**: If the scene has a high contrast between bright and dark areas, use the HDR feature to capture more detail in both the highlights and shadows.

3. Sports Mode

What It Is: Sports mode is designed for capturing fast-moving subjects. It optimizes the camera's settings to freeze motion, making it ideal for photographing sports events, wildlife, or any scene with quick movement.

How It Works:

- The camera selects a fast shutter speed to freeze action.
- It may increase ISO if needed to maintain proper exposure with the fast shutter.
- The autofocus is set to continuous mode to track moving subjects effectively.

Tips for Sports Mode:

- **Shoot in Burst Mode**: The Canon EOS R50 has a burst or continuous shooting option. Using this with Sports Mode allows you to capture multiple frames per second, increasing your chances of getting a sharp shot of a fast-moving subject.
- **Positioning**: Try to anticipate where the action will be, and position yourself accordingly.

- **Zoom Lens**: If you're photographing distant subjects, use a zoom lens for better reach and more dynamic shots.

4. Night Scene Mode

What It Is: Night Scene mode helps you capture low-light images with balanced exposure. This mode is ideal for shooting in dark environments, such as nighttime cityscapes or indoor settings with dim lighting.

How It Works:

- The camera may use a slower shutter speed to gather more light.
- It can adjust ISO to brighten the image while managing noise.
- Night Scene mode might also adjust white balance to maintain natural colors under artificial lighting.

Tips for Night Scene Mode:

- **Stabilize Your Camera**: Slow shutter speeds can cause motion blur, so use a tripod or rest the camera on a stable surface.
- **Avoid Flash**: Night Scene Mode usually avoids flash to capture the natural ambiance of the scene. If you need extra light, try using a handheld LED light for subtle illumination.
- **Use Exposure Compensation**: Night shots can sometimes look too bright if the camera overexposes. Use exposure compensation to darken the image slightly if needed.

Creative Filters

Creative Filters are preset effects that you can apply directly in-camera, allowing you to experiment with different artistic looks. Using these filters, you can add creative flair to your photos without needing additional editing software. Below are some of the most popular Creative Filters available on the Canon EOS R50.

1. Grainy Black & White

What It Is: This filter converts your image to black and white with added grain, simulating the look of high-ISO film. This effect is perfect for creating a vintage or documentary-style appearance.

How It Works:

- The camera removes all color from the image.
- It adds simulated film grain for texture and an old-fashioned feel.

- Contrast is often increased, emphasizing light and shadow.

Tips for Grainy Black & White:

- **Use in High-Contrast Scenes**: This filter works well when there is strong contrast, as it highlights the difference between light and dark areas.
- **Subject Matter**: This filter is great for street photography or portraits, where the grainy texture can add mood and drama.

2. Soft Focus

What It Is: The Soft Focus filter blurs the image slightly to create a dreamy, ethereal effect. This filter is ideal for portraits or romantic landscapes.

How It Works:

- The camera reduces sharpness and may add a slight glow around highlights.
- Contrast is often softened to create a gentle, delicate appearance.

Tips for Soft Focus:

- **Portraits and Nature Shots**: This filter is well-suited for portraits and nature scenes where a soft, dream-like quality enhances the subject.
- **Avoid Overuse**: Use Soft Focus sparingly to avoid making the image appear overly blurry or lacking in detail.

3. Toy Camera Effect

What It Is: The Toy Camera effect mimics the appearance of images taken with old toy cameras. It typically adds vignetting (darkening around the edges) and enhances color saturation.

How It Works:

- Colors are enhanced to look more saturated and vibrant.
- A vignette effect is applied, focusing attention on the center of the image.

Tips for Toy Camera Effect:

- **Urban Photography**: This effect can add a nostalgic, playful look to urban scenes, making it suitable for street photography.
- **Subjects with Bright Colors**: The saturation boost is especially effective with colorful subjects, making them stand out.

4. Miniature Effect

What It Is: The Miniature effect makes real-life scenes appear like miniature models by selectively blurring parts of the image, simulating the look of tilt-shift photography.

How It Works:

- The camera applies selective blur to areas above and below a specific focus point, creating a shallow depth of field effect.
- Colors may be slightly enhanced to add to the "miniature" feel.

Tips for Miniature Effect:

- **Use with Overhead Shots**: This filter works best with overhead shots of scenes like city streets or landscapes, where the blur can mimic the shallow depth of field seen in macro photography.
- **Adjust the Focus Area**: Experiment with where you place the focus point, as this will affect which part of the image remains sharp.

5. Fish-Eye Effect

What It Is: The Fish-Eye effect distorts the image to create a rounded, wide-angle look, similar to what you'd get with a dedicated fish-eye lens.

How It Works:

- The camera applies distortion to make the center of the image appear closer and the edges appear curved.
- Colors are typically enhanced to make the effect more striking.

Tips for Fish-Eye Effect:

- **Close-Up Shots**: This effect can be fun for close-up shots of objects or faces, as it exaggerates shapes.
- **Experiment with Compositions**: Fish-Eye creates a highly distorted look, so use it for creative or humorous images rather than for standard photography.

Conclusion

Scene Modes and Creative Filters on the Canon EOS R50 are excellent tools for photographers who want quick access to settings tailored to specific types of shots and creative effects. Scene Modes, such as Portrait, Landscape, Sports, and Night Scene, take the guesswork out of complex adjustments, allowing beginners to achieve professional-looking results with minimal effort.

Creative Filters, like Grainy Black & White, Soft Focus, and Miniature Effect, provide fun and artistic options that can transform your images right in the camera. Whether you're capturing everyday moments or exploring new styles, these modes and filters add versatility and creativity to your photography without requiring extensive post-processing skills. Experimenting with each mode and filter can help you discover new ways to express your vision through photography.

Using the HDR and Panorama Features

The Canon EOS R50 includes HDR (High Dynamic Range) and Panorama shooting features that help photographers capture scenes that may otherwise be difficult to photograph. HDR is ideal for scenes with a lot of contrast between light and dark areas, while Panorama allows you to capture wide, sweeping landscapes or large architectural scenes in a single shot. Both features enhance your creative options, making it easier to capture high-quality, dynamic images without needing extensive post-processing.

In this section, we'll explore how the HDR and Panorama features work, when to use them, and provide step-by-step guides on how to achieve the best results with your Canon EOS R50.

Understanding HDR (High Dynamic Range)

HDR, or High Dynamic Range, is a feature that captures multiple exposures of the same scene, combining them into one image that balances both the bright and dark areas. This process is especially helpful in situations where there's a high contrast between highlights (bright areas) and shadows (dark areas). By combining multiple images, HDR creates a final image that shows more detail throughout the tonal range, making it look more true-to-life.

How HDR Works

1. **Multiple Exposures**: When you activate HDR on the Canon EOS R50, the camera takes multiple shots (usually three) of the same scene at different exposures.

2. **Combining Images**: The camera automatically merges these images into one composite photo. It takes the best-exposed parts of each image and blends them to create a balanced final photo.

3. **Final Result**: The resulting image has more detail in the highlights and shadows, producing a well-exposed photo that captures a greater range of tones.

When to Use HDR

HDR is particularly effective in the following situations:

- **Landscape Photography**: Landscapes often contain bright skies and dark foregrounds. HDR balances the exposure to capture details in both.

- **Architecture**: When photographing buildings with shadows and sunlight, HDR can reveal details in both the shaded and well-lit areas.
- **Sunrises and Sunsets**: These scenes typically have intense lighting variations. HDR helps preserve details in both the bright sky and the darker foreground.

Step-by-Step Guide to Using HDR on the Canon EOS R50

1. **Activate HDR Mode**:

   Go to the camera's menu and select the HDR mode. You'll usually find it under the shooting settings.

2. **Choose HDR Settings**:

   The Canon EOS R50 may offer options to adjust the strength of the HDR effect (e.g., Natural, Art Standard, Art Vivid). Start with "Natural" for a balanced look, and explore other settings as you gain experience.

3. **Set Up Your Shot**:

   HDR works best when the camera is steady, so consider using a tripod. Position your camera to capture the desired scene.

4. **Frame and Shoot**:

   Press the shutter button to take the HDR photo. The camera will automatically capture multiple exposures and process them into one image.

5. **Review and Save**:

   After taking the shot, review the image to see if it meets your expectations. HDR mode typically creates a JPEG file, even if you're shooting in RAW, as the camera has already processed the image.

Tips for Better HDR Photography

- **Use a Tripod**: Since HDR involves multiple exposures, any movement between shots can cause blur. A tripod ensures stability.
- **Avoid HDR with Moving Subjects**: HDR is best for static scenes. Moving elements, like people or animals, can create "ghosting" (blurred edges) in the final image.
- **Experiment with HDR Strength**: Start with the "Natural" HDR mode to keep the image looking realistic. Other modes can create a more stylized effect, but may sometimes look unnatural.

Understanding the Panorama Feature

The Panorama feature allows you to capture wide scenes by stitching together multiple images into a single, elongated image. This is useful for photographing large landscapes, cityscapes, or any scene that doesn't fit within a standard frame. The Panorama function captures the scene as you move the camera horizontally (or vertically, in some cases), creating a seamless, sweeping image.

How Panorama Works

1. **Continuous Shooting**: When you enable Panorama mode, the Canon EOS R50 guides you to pan the camera across the scene. It captures a series of images as you move.

2. **Image Stitching**: The camera automatically combines the images to create one panoramic photo.

3. **Final Result**: The resulting panorama covers a wider angle than a single image, capturing more of the scene in one shot.

When to Use Panorama

The Panorama feature is ideal for:

- **Landscapes**: When you're photographing mountains, oceans, or fields, a single photo often doesn't capture the full scene. Panorama provides a wider perspective.

- **Cityscapes and Architecture**: For photographing city skylines or large buildings, Panorama captures the scene's full width.

- **Interior Spaces**: In tight spaces, like rooms or corridors, Panorama can provide a sense of the entire space by including more of the environment.

Step-by-Step Guide to Using Panorama on the Canon EOS R50

1. **Switch to Panorama Mode**:

   In the Canon EOS R50's shooting mode, select "Panorama" mode. This can usually be found in the Scene or Special Effects menu.

2. **Choose Your Direction**:

   Select the direction in which you'll be panning the camera (left-to-right, right-to-left, or up-to-down). Choose the direction that best fits the scene.

3. **Start Capturing**:

Press the shutter button and slowly pan the camera in the chosen direction. The camera will guide you to move at a steady pace.

4. **Complete the Panorama**:

Continue panning until the camera has captured the full scene or until you release the shutter button. The camera will then process and stitch the images together.

5. **Review the Panorama**:

Check the final image to ensure the scene is captured smoothly and without any gaps or alignment issues.

Tips for Better Panorama Photography

- **Move Steadily**: Keep a smooth, steady pace as you pan to avoid uneven stitching.
- **Avoid Overlapping Motion**: Moving objects, such as people or vehicles, can create inconsistencies when stitching images. Try to capture scenes with minimal movement.
- **Use Wide-Angle Lenses Carefully**: While Panorama mode can expand a scene, using an ultra-wide-angle lens can sometimes distort the edges. Choose a lens that complements the scene's size and scale.

Practical Tips for HDR and Panorama

- **HDR and Panorama Together**: The Canon EOS R50 may not support HDR within Panorama mode. If you need both, capture separate images for each effect and combine them in post-processing software.
- **Use a Tripod for Both Modes**: Stability is essential for HDR and Panorama, as both rely on precise alignment. A tripod ensures consistent framing.
- **Mind the Lighting**: HDR works best in scenes with mixed lighting, while Panorama is better suited to evenly lit scenes to prevent inconsistencies across stitched frames.

Conclusion

The HDR and Panorama features on the Canon EOS R50 offer valuable tools for photographers looking to capture complex scenes with ease. HDR brings out details in high-contrast settings by combining multiple exposures, while Panorama stitches multiple images into a single, sweeping view, perfect for expansive landscapes or architectural scenes. Both features enhance your creative options, allowing you to capture images that would be challenging with a single shot.

Experimenting with HDR and Panorama can open up new possibilities in your photography, enabling you to capture dynamic and immersive images. With practice, you'll be able to identify the perfect moments to use these features, adding depth and creativity to your Canon EOS R50 photography experience

CHAPTER 6

ADVANCED PHOTOGRAPHY TECHNIQUES

Long Exposure and Night Photography

Capturing long exposure and night photography can bring a new level of creativity to your images. With long exposure, you can create striking effects like light trails, silky smooth water, or bright starry skies. This section covers essential concepts of long exposure and night photography using the Canon EOS R50, explaining each aspect simply for both beginners and professionals.

Understanding Long Exposure and Night Photography

Long exposure photography involves using slower shutter speeds to capture an image over an extended period of time. This technique allows you to create dramatic effects with moving subjects. For instance, you can capture the light trails of cars moving through a street or create an impression of smooth water in a flowing river.

Night photography is closely related to long exposure, as shooting in low-light conditions requires slower shutter speeds to allow more light into the camera. Night photography can be used to capture breathtaking images of cityscapes, star trails, or even the moon. However, taking quality night photos with a low noise level and sharp details requires some knowledge of exposure and camera settings.

Key Concepts for Long Exposure and Night Photography

1. **Shutter Speed**

    - Shutter speed determines how long the camera sensor is exposed to light. In long exposure photography, slower shutter speeds are used, such as 1 second, 10 seconds, or even minutes.

    - For night photography, you typically need to extend the shutter speed to let in more light since low-light scenes require more exposure time for details to be visible.

    - On the Canon EOS R50, the shutter speed can be adjusted in various modes like Manual (M), Aperture Priority (Av), and Shutter Priority (Tv), giving you flexibility in creative control.

2. **Aperture**

- Aperture controls the amount of light that enters the camera through the lens. A wider aperture (e.g., f/2.8) allows more light into the sensor, which is useful in low-light conditions.

- In night photography, a wider aperture will help you capture more detail with a faster shutter speed, while a smaller aperture (e.g., f/11) may be more appropriate for long exposure landscape shots to get everything in focus.

- Balancing aperture with shutter speed is critical in night photography; this combination helps to avoid overly bright or too-dark shots.

3. **ISO**

    - ISO controls the sensitivity of the camera's sensor to light. A higher ISO allows you to capture more light, but it also increases the noise (graininess) in the image.

    - For night photography, an ISO range between 800 to 3200 can be helpful on the Canon EOS R50, depending on the available light. A lower ISO will yield less noise, but it may also require a longer shutter speed or wider aperture to balance exposure.

    - Finding the right ISO setting is key to achieving a sharp image without too much grain, especially in dark environments.

4. **Focus and Stability**

    - In long exposure and night photography, focusing is critical, as even slight shifts can result in blurred images. Manual focus can be particularly useful in dark scenes since the camera's autofocus may struggle to lock onto subjects in low light.

    - Using a tripod is essential to keep the camera stable during long exposures, preventing motion blur that occurs from camera shake. The Canon EOS R50's **Image Stabilization** can help reduce minor vibrations, but for exposures longer than 1/10th of a second, a tripod is highly recommended.

    - Consider using a remote shutter release or the Canon Camera Connect app to avoid any shake caused by pressing the shutter button.

5. **Noise Reduction**

    - Long exposure and night photography can create noise, especially in darker areas. The Canon EOS R50 offers in-camera **long exposure noise reduction** settings that reduce noise automatically during long exposures.

- You can enable noise reduction in the menu settings, although it will slightly increase the processing time for each photo. This is a trade-off for a cleaner image, especially useful when shooting starry skies or dark cityscapes.

Step-by-Step Guide to Long Exposure and Night Photography

Step 1: Set Up Your Camera on a Stable Surface

Mount your Canon EOS R50 on a sturdy tripod to prevent any camera shake. A tripod is essential, as long exposures will capture any movement of the camera as blur, affecting the sharpness of the final image.

Step 2: Choose Your Camera Mode and Settings

For greater control, set your camera to **Manual (M)** mode. This mode allows you to adjust the shutter speed, aperture, and ISO independently. In Manual mode, you can fine-tune each setting to achieve the desired effect.

Alternatively, use **Shutter Priority (Tv)** if you want the camera to automatically adjust the aperture based on your chosen shutter speed. This mode can be helpful for beginners to manage exposure without adjusting too many settings manually.

Step 3: Set the Shutter Speed

For long exposures, set a slower shutter speed to allow more light to reach the sensor. Typical shutter speeds for long exposure photography range from 1 second to 30 seconds or even longer, depending on the scene.

- **Light trails (e.g., cars on a highway)**: Start with a shutter speed of around 10–30 seconds to capture continuous trails.
- **Smooth water**: Use a shutter speed of 2–5 seconds to create a silky effect on rivers or ocean waves.
- **Stars and night sky**: For star trails, try 15–30 seconds or experiment with the Bulb mode (B) for exposures lasting several minutes.

Step 4: Adjust the Aperture

Select a wider aperture (smaller f-stop number, like f/2.8 to f/4) to capture more light in low-light scenes. For cityscapes and landscapes, consider a smaller aperture (larger f-stop, like f/11 or f/16) to keep more elements in focus. Adjusting the aperture will affect how much of the scene appears sharp.

Step 5: Set the ISO

Start with a low ISO (such as ISO 100 or 200) for better image quality, particularly when there's still some ambient light. As it gets darker, you may need to increase the ISO (800–3200) to balance the exposure. Use the lowest ISO setting that still gives a bright enough image to minimize noise.

Step 6: Focus Manually

Switch to **Manual Focus** to ensure the focus doesn't shift accidentally. Use the camera's live view mode to magnify and focus on a specific part of the scene. In low-light situations, focusing on bright points like stars or distant streetlights can be helpful.

Step 7: Enable Long Exposure Noise Reduction (Optional)

Enable **Long Exposure Noise Reduction** in your camera settings to reduce graininess, especially for exposures longer than 1 second. Keep in mind this will lengthen the processing time after each shot, so plan accordingly if you're taking multiple photos.

Step 8: Use a Remote Shutter or Timer

Use a **remote shutter release** or set the **2-second self-timer** to avoid any camera movement from pressing the shutter button. If you have the Canon Camera Connect app, you can control the shutter from your smartphone for hands-free shooting.

Tips for Success in Long Exposure and Night Photography

- **Scout Your Location**: Look for interesting sources of light, like streetlights or stars, which can add depth and interest to your composition.
- **Monitor the Exposure**: Use the **exposure meter** in the Canon EOS R50's viewfinder or live view to gauge the brightness of your scene.
- **Experiment with Different Shutter Speeds**: Adjust shutter speed to get different effects with motion. For example, a longer shutter speed will increase the length of light trails or make waves appear even smoother.
- **Check for Overexposure**: In night photography, light sources (like streetlights) can cause overexposure. Use the camera's **Highlight Alert** feature to check for overexposed areas, and adjust your settings if necessary.
- **Practice and Experiment**: Long exposure photography requires patience and experimentation. Try different shutter speeds, compositions, and light sources to develop a unique style.

Conclusion

Long exposure and night photography open up new creative possibilities, from capturing mesmerizing light trails to showcasing a calm, starlit night sky. With practice, the Canon EOS R50 can become an excellent tool for both beginners and professionals looking to master low-light photography. By understanding and controlling the essential settings—shutter speed, aperture, ISO, focus, and stability—you can take stunning, high-quality images that showcase the beauty of low-light scenes.

Using Focus Bracketing and Stacking

Focus bracketing and stacking are powerful techniques that allow you to achieve a greater depth of field in your photos, making every part of the subject appear sharp and in focus. This technique is especially useful for macro photography, landscape photography, and other close-up scenes where you want fine details to be clearly visible across different focal planes. The Canon EOS R50's focus bracketing feature is straightforward and accessible for both beginners and professionals, making it easier than ever to create images with exceptional clarity.

Understanding Focus Bracketing and Stacking

Focus Bracketing involves taking multiple images of the same scene but with different focus points. The camera shifts focus gradually from the nearest point to the farthest, capturing several shots with varied focal planes.

Focus Stacking is the process of blending or merging these bracketed shots together using software to create a single image where every focal plane is sharp. When combined, these techniques allow photographers to capture images with incredible depth of field that would be difficult or impossible to achieve in a single shot.

Key Concepts for Using Focus Bracketing and Stacking

1. **Depth of Field**

   - Depth of field refers to the portion of the image that appears in sharp focus. In a single image, depth of field can be limited, especially in close-up or macro photography. With focus stacking, you can capture all parts of the subject in focus by blending images taken at different focal points.

   - The Canon EOS R50 allows you to set the bracketing parameters, so you can control the starting and ending focus distances, giving you flexibility to cover the entire depth of the subject.

2. **Focus Shift and Increment Settings**

   - Focus shift is the adjustment of focus between each shot in the focus bracketing sequence. The increment setting determines how much the focus changes from one shot to the next. Larger increments cover more distance between shots, while smaller increments provide finer detail in close-up work.

- The Canon EOS R50 lets you customize these increments, which is helpful for different types of photography. For macro shots, use a small increment for fine detail, whereas larger increments work well for landscapes.

3. **Stable Shooting and Lighting Conditions**
    - Stable shooting conditions are crucial for successful focus bracketing. Any movement of the camera or the subject can cause misalignment, making it difficult to stack the images later. Using a tripod and remote shutter release will help avoid camera shake.
    - Consistent lighting is also important because variations in lighting can cause inconsistencies when stacking images. For beginners, natural lighting or a continuous light source is usually easier to control than flash.

4. **Post-Processing for Focus Stacking**
    - After capturing a set of bracketed images, the next step is to merge them using focus-stacking software, such as Adobe Photoshop, Helicon Focus, or specialized Canon software.
    - This process combines the sharpest parts of each image, resulting in one fully focused image. Beginners can follow straightforward tutorials to learn the basics of stacking, while professionals may explore advanced settings for refined control over blending layers.

Step-by-Step Guide to Focus Bracketing and Stacking

Step 1: Prepare Your Scene and Camera Setup

Set up your Canon EOS R50 on a sturdy tripod. This ensures that your camera remains stable throughout the series of focus-bracketed shots. Position your subject and ensure adequate, even lighting, especially if shooting indoors. A consistent light source, like a softbox or diffused natural light, can help maintain uniformity across your shots.

Step 2: Set the Camera to Focus Bracketing Mode

- **Navigate to the Focus Bracketing Setting**: Go to the camera's menu and locate the focus bracketing option. Select **Enable** to activate this feature.
- **Adjust Bracketing Settings**: You will be able to set parameters such as the **number of shots** and the **focus increment**.
    - **Number of Shots**: This determines how many images will be taken with progressively adjusted focus. For macro photography, more shots are generally

needed due to the shallow depth of field, while fewer shots may suffice for landscapes.

- o **Focus Increment**: This sets the amount of focus shift between each shot. Start with a smaller increment for close-up shots to capture finer details and a larger increment for distant subjects.

Step 3: Set Aperture and ISO

Choose an **aperture** that provides a balance between depth of field and sharpness. For close-up or macro shots, a slightly smaller aperture (such as f/8 or f/11) can help achieve more detail, but keep in mind that very small apertures (e.g., f/16 or smaller) may introduce diffraction, which reduces image sharpness.

Set the **ISO** to the lowest possible setting, such as ISO 100, to maintain image quality. A low ISO helps avoid noise, which can interfere with stacking results.

Step 4: Start the Focus Bracketing Sequence

Once all settings are in place:

- Use the **Manual Focus** option to set the initial focus point on the closest part of the subject.

- Trigger the camera using either a remote shutter release or a timer to prevent any movement. This will start the focus bracketing sequence, capturing each shot with slight adjustments in focus.

The Canon EOS R50 will automatically take the series of bracketed images according to the settings you defined. If your camera doesn't automatically bracket, you can manually adjust the focus slightly between each shot, but this approach may require practice.

Step 5: Review the Captured Images

After completing the bracketed shots, review them on the camera's display to ensure all focal points have been captured. Look for any missed focus areas; if you notice gaps, you may need to redo the sequence with adjustments in increment or shot count.

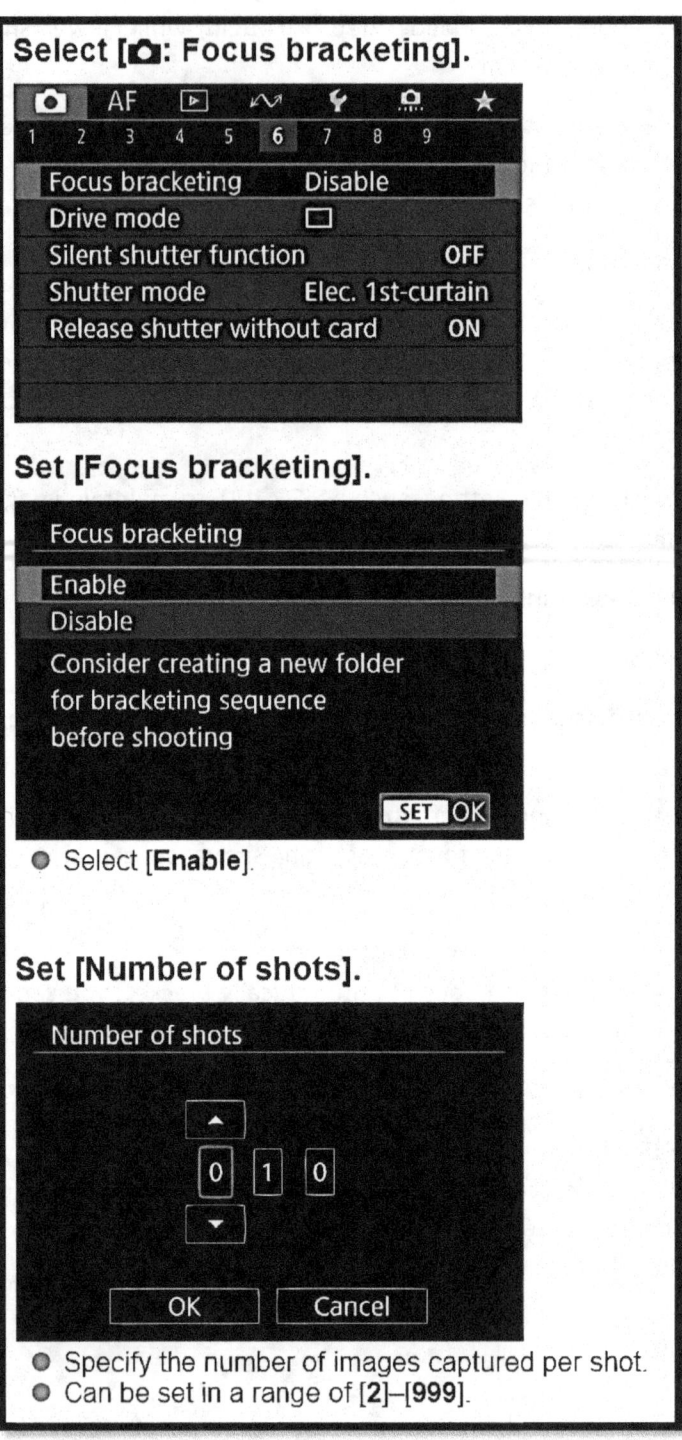

Set [Focus increment].

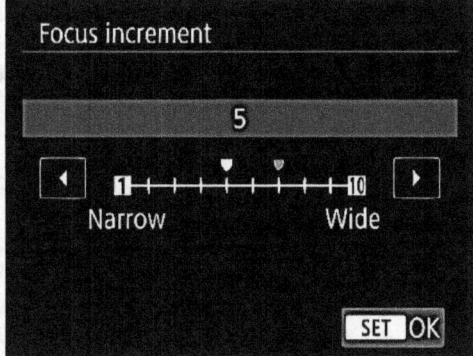

- Specify how much to shift the focus. This amount is automatically adjusted to suit the aperture value at the time of shooting.
Larger aperture values increase the focus shift and make focus bracketing cover a wider range under the same focus increment and number of shots.
- After completing the settings, press the <⊛> button.

Set [Exposure smoothing].

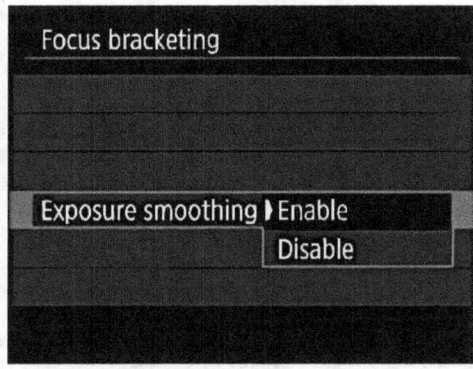

- You can compensate for changes in image brightness during focus bracketing by selecting [**Enable**], so that the camera makes adjustments based on differences between the displayed and actual aperture value (effective f/number), which varies by focal position.
- Select [**Disable**] if you prefer not to compensate for changes in image brightness during focus bracketing. Use this option for purposes other than depth compositing of the captured images in applications such as DPP.

Set [Depth composite].

- Select [**Enable**] for in-camera depth compositing. The depth-composited image is saved.
- Select [**Disable**] if you prefer not to perform in-camera depth compositing. Only captured images are saved.

> **Caution**

Set [Crop depth comp.].

- Select [**Enable**] for cropping before compositing, to prepare any images without a sufficient angle of view for compositing alignment by cropping them to correct the angle of view.
- Select [**Disable**] if you prefer not to crop these images. In this case, areas without a sufficient angle of view are covered by a black border in the saved images. You can crop the images manually or edit them as needed.

Take the picture.

- To save your shots in a new folder, tap [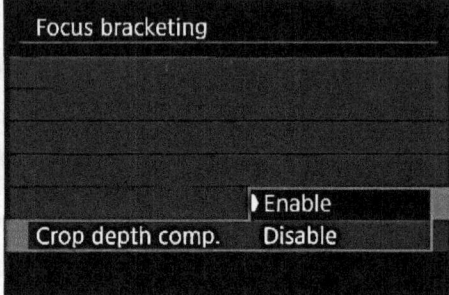] and select [**OK**].
- Focus at the nearer end of your preferred focal range, then press the shutter button completely.
- Once shooting begins, release the shutter button.
- The camera shoots continuously, shifting the focal position toward infinity.
- Shooting ends after your specified number of images, or at the far end of the focal range.
- To cancel shooting, press the shutter button completely again.

Post-Processing: Stacking Your Focus-Bracketed Images

Once you've captured the bracketed images, the next step is to stack them using image-editing software. Here's a breakdown of the stacking process in Adobe Photoshop, one of the most popular tools for focus stacking.

Step 1: Import the Images into Photoshop

- Open Adobe Photoshop and go to **File > Scripts > Load Files into Stack**.
- Select all the bracketed images you want to stack, then click **OK**. Photoshop will open each image in a separate layer.

Step 2: Align the Layers

Even with a tripod, slight shifts can occur. To align the images:

- Select all layers in the Layers panel.
- Go to **Edit > Auto-Align Layers** and choose **Auto**. This will align all layers, minimizing any small shifts between images.

Step 3: Apply Focus Stacking

- With all layers still selected, go to **Edit > Auto-Blend Layers**.
- Select **Stack Images** and make sure **Seamless Tones and Colors** is checked. Click **OK**.
- Photoshop will blend the sharpest parts of each layer, creating a single, fully-focused image.

Step 4: Final Adjustments

Once the stacked image is created, you can make final adjustments:

- Crop to remove any misaligned edges from stacking.
- Use adjustment layers for brightness, contrast, or color correction to fine-tune the appearance.

Practical Applications of Focus Bracketing and Stacking

- **Macro Photography**: Focus stacking is widely used in macro photography, where close-up shots of flowers, insects, or textures require extensive detail. The shallow depth of field inherent in macro shots can make it difficult to keep all parts of the subject in focus, making focus stacking ideal.

- **Landscape Photography**: In landscape photography, you may want the foreground, middle ground, and background all sharply focused. Focus stacking allows for this, enabling a crisp view of distant mountains, foreground rocks, and other elements within one frame.

- **Product Photography**: For e-commerce or catalog images, product photography requires a high level of detail across the entire subject. Focus bracketing and stacking help maintain sharpness and highlight product features clearly.

Tips for Success in Focus Bracketing and Stacking

- **Start with a Few Shots**: For beginners, start with a smaller number of bracketed shots to get used to the process. Once comfortable, you can experiment with more images for finer detail.

- **Use Consistent Lighting**: Avoid variable lighting conditions. If possible, use a continuous light source or shoot in natural, even lighting to avoid variations in color and exposure.

- **Practice Patience**: Focus stacking can take time and patience, especially in post-processing. Experiment with different subjects and settings to become familiar with the technique.

- **Experiment with Different Focal Lengths**: Focus bracketing isn't limited to macro photography; try using different focal lengths to explore its effects in various contexts, from close-up shots to wide-angle landscapes.

Conclusion

Focus bracketing and stacking are excellent techniques for creating images with impressive detail and depth of field. With the Canon EOS R50, beginners and professionals alike can harness these methods to capture stunningly sharp images, regardless of the limitations of single-shot depth of field. By carefully setting up your camera, adjusting the focus increment and shot count, and using post-processing software, you can unlock new levels of creativity in photography. With practice and experimentation, focus bracketing and stacking will become valuable tools in your photographic toolkit.

High-Speed Burst and Action Shots

Capturing action shots requires a special set of techniques to freeze fast-moving subjects and deliver sharp, exciting images. Whether you're photographing athletes in motion, wildlife, or even playful children, the **high-speed burst** mode on the Canon EOS R50 allows you to take a rapid series of shots in quick succession, maximizing your chances of getting the perfect shot. This feature, combined with the R50's fast autofocus and customizable settings, makes action photography accessible to beginners while providing flexibility for professionals to achieve creative, dynamic results.

Key Concepts of High-Speed Burst and Action Photography

1. **Shutter Speed**

    Shutter speed is the most critical setting for capturing action shots. A fast shutter speed freezes motion, while a slower speed can create intentional blur that emphasizes movement. For action shots, aim for a shutter speed of at least **1/500th of a second** or faster, depending on the speed of your subject. For faster subjects, like athletes or cars, speeds of **1/1000th** or **1/2000th of a second** are ideal.

2. **High-Speed Burst Mode**

    In high-speed burst mode, the Canon EOS R50 captures multiple images in rapid succession. This mode is perfect for action scenes where the moment can change in an instant. By holding down the shutter button, you take a sequence of photos at high speed, which increases your chances of getting a sharp, well-timed shot. The R50's burst rate of up to **15 frames per second** in electronic shutter mode means you can capture every phase of a movement.

3. **Autofocus (AF) Tracking and Continuous AF Mode**

    When shooting action, autofocus (AF) tracking is essential to keep moving subjects in focus. The Canon EOS R50 offers **continuous AF** mode, which continuously adjusts focus as your subject moves. Using the camera's **AF tracking** capabilities, you can lock onto a subject, allowing the camera to follow and maintain focus on it as it moves through the frame. This is particularly helpful for fast-moving subjects, such as animals, children, or athletes.

4. **ISO and Aperture**

    Balancing ISO and aperture is necessary to maintain good exposure when using high shutter speeds. Because fast shutter speeds limit the amount of light entering the camera, you may need to increase the ISO or widen the aperture (e.g., to f/2.8 or f/4) to capture a well-lit image. Increasing the ISO can introduce some noise, but the Canon EOS R50's sensor does an excellent job of minimizing it, especially in well-lit environments.

5. **Panning Technique**

    For dynamic action shots, you can try the **panning technique**, where you move the camera along with your subject as it moves. This keeps the subject relatively sharp while blurring the background, emphasizing the sense of motion. Panning can be challenging but adds a unique touch to action photos, giving them a cinematic feel.

Step-by-Step Guide to Capturing High-Speed Burst and Action Shots

Step 1: Set Up High-Speed Burst Mode

1. **Select the Burst Mode on the Canon EOS R50**:
    - Press the **Drive** button or go to the **Shooting Mode** menu to choose the high-speed burst mode. Select **High-Speed Continuous Shooting** for the fastest burst rate.
    - Once selected, holding down the shutter button will capture multiple frames per second, allowing you to photograph rapid movements.

2. **Adjust Shutter Speed for Action**:
    - Switch to **Shutter Priority (Tv) mode** on the Canon EOS R50, which allows you to set the shutter speed while the camera automatically adjusts other settings for optimal exposure.
    - Start with a shutter speed of **1/500th of a second** for moderate action and go faster if your subject is moving quickly.

Step 2: Set Autofocus for Moving Subjects

1. **Choose Continuous AF (AI Servo) Mode**:

    Go to the **AF settings** in the menu and select **AI Servo AF** (Continuous AF). This mode allows the camera to keep focusing on a moving subject, ensuring that it remains sharp as it moves across the frame.

2. **Use Subject Tracking AF**:
    - For more reliable results, activate **Subject Tracking** in the AF settings. This feature allows you to lock onto a subject, and the Canon EOS R50 will continue to follow and keep it in focus as long as you're holding down the shutter button halfway.
    - For beginners, practice locking onto a slower subject, such as a person walking, before moving to faster-moving subjects like animals or sports.

Step 3: Set ISO and Aperture for Optimal Exposure

1. **Adjust the ISO**:
    - Set your ISO to a level that maintains good exposure without introducing too much noise. If you're shooting in daylight, ISO 100 or 200 is ideal. For indoor or lower-light situations, you may need to raise the ISO to **800** or even higher.

- The Canon EOS R50 has a reliable ISO performance, but always aim to keep ISO as low as possible for the sharpest image quality.

2. **Choose a Wide Aperture**:

    To allow more light to enter the camera, set your aperture to a wider setting, such as **f/2.8** or **f/4**. This also helps create a shallow depth of field, making your subject stand out against a slightly blurred background, which is appealing in action shots.

Step 4: Consider the Panning Technique for Enhanced Motion

1. **Set a Slightly Slower Shutter Speed**:

    For panning shots, select a slightly slower shutter speed, around **1/60th to 1/125th of a second**, depending on the speed of your subject. This speed will blur the background while maintaining enough sharpness on the subject.

2. **Match Your Subject's Movement**:

    - Stand steadily and start tracking your subject in the viewfinder before pressing the shutter button. As the subject moves, smoothly pan your camera to match its motion while pressing and holding the shutter button.
    - Continue panning even after the burst sequence ends to avoid abrupt movements that could result in uneven blur.

Step 5: Capture Multiple Shots for the Perfect Frame

1. **Anticipate Key Moments**:

    Think ahead and try to anticipate moments of peak action, such as a runner jumping or a bird taking off. The high-speed burst mode will help you capture a sequence of frames, but timing can still improve your chances of getting the perfect shot.

2. **Hold Down the Shutter Button**:

    When you're ready, press and hold the shutter button to activate the burst mode. The Canon EOS R50 will rapidly capture frames, providing a series of images that you can review and choose from later.

Practical Applications of High-Speed Burst and Action Shots

1. **Sports Photography**:

    High-speed burst is widely used in sports to capture athletes in motion, from runners to basketball players. By using fast shutter speeds, you can freeze movements, like a soccer player mid-kick, and get crisp, detailed shots that highlight the intensity of the sport.

2. **Wildlife Photography**:

    Wildlife is often unpredictable, and animals tend to move quickly. High-speed burst allows you to capture behaviors and actions, like a bird in flight or a fox running, without missing the moment. Tracking AF is especially useful here, as it helps maintain focus on fast, erratic movement.

3. **Everyday Action**:

    High-speed burst isn't limited to sports or wildlife. It's great for everyday action shots too, such as children playing or pets running in the yard. These spontaneous moments can be challenging to capture without a burst sequence.

Tips for Success in High-Speed Burst and Action Photography

- **Practice AF Tracking**: Tracking moving subjects takes practice, especially if they're fast. Spend time practicing on slower subjects, such as people walking or dogs running, before tackling faster subjects.

- **Use a Fast Memory Card**: Shooting in burst mode generates a lot of data quickly. A fast SD card with a high write speed will prevent the camera from slowing down and ensure smooth capture without delays.

- **Experiment with Burst Length**: In some cases, a short burst of 3-5 frames may be enough, while in others, a longer burst is better. Experiment to see what gives you the best results.

- **Review and Select the Best Shots**: Action photography can produce dozens of images. Reviewing and selecting the best frames afterward will allow you to choose the moment with the best composition, focus, and exposure.

Troubleshooting Common Issues in Action Photography

- **Blurry Images**: If your images come out blurry, your shutter speed may be too slow. Increase it to freeze the action more effectively.

- **Out-of-Focus Subjects**: If the subject is not in focus, ensure you're using Continuous AF and subject tracking to keep it sharp.

- **Noise in Low Light**: In low light, using a higher ISO might introduce noise. For best results, try shooting in well-lit conditions, or use software to reduce noise in post-processing.

Conclusion

High-speed burst and action photography allow you to capture moments that are gone in a split second. With the Canon EOS R50, beginners and professionals alike have the tools to create sharp, dynamic images that convey the excitement of fast-moving subjects. By mastering settings such as shutter speed, continuous AF, and ISO, and incorporating techniques like panning, you can achieve stunning action shots that tell a story.

CHAPTER 7

WORKING WITH LENSES AND ACCESSORIES

Lens Compatibility and Mount Adapter Options

The Canon EOS R50 is part of Canon's mirrorless lineup, using the versatile **RF lens mount**. Choosing the right lens opens up a world of creative possibilities, allowing you to capture everything from sweeping landscapes to detailed portraits. However, understanding which lenses are compatible and when to use a mount adapter is essential, especially if you're considering Canon's other lens series, like the EF or EF-S lenses.

This chapter covers how lens compatibility works on the EOS R50, how to choose lenses that suit your photography needs, and how to use mount adapters effectively.

Understanding Lens Compatibility on the Canon EOS R50

1. **The RF Lens Mount**

    - The EOS R50, like other cameras in Canon's mirrorless R series, uses the **RF mount**. This mount was introduced with Canon's mirrorless cameras and is designed for optimal performance, including **fast autofocus**, **high-quality image capture**, and **efficient electronic communication** between the lens and the camera body.

    - RF lenses are specifically built to make the most of the mirrorless design, with a **shorter flange distance** (the space between the lens mount and the sensor) than Canon's older EF and EF-S lenses used on DSLRs. This shorter distance improves optical performance, making RF lenses ideal for mirrorless cameras like the EOS R50.

2. **Native RF Lenses**

    - **RF lenses** are designed exclusively for Canon's mirrorless RF mount cameras, including the R50. These lenses offer advanced features such as **smooth and quick autofocus**, high-quality optics, and **customizable control rings** that allow you to adjust settings directly on the lens.

    - RF lenses are available in a wide range of focal lengths and types, including **zoom, prime, macro, and telephoto** lenses. These options make it possible to shoot various styles and subjects, from close-up macro photography to distant wildlife scenes.

- When using RF lenses on the EOS R50, there is no need for any mount adapter, as these lenses are natively compatible with the camera's RF mount.

3. **EF and EF-S Lenses**

    - Canon's **EF and EF-S lenses** were designed for Canon DSLR cameras, which use the EF mount (for full-frame cameras) and EF-S mount (for crop-sensor cameras). If you already own EF or EF-S lenses from a Canon DSLR, you can still use these lenses on the EOS R50 with an **adapter**.

    - **EF lenses** cover the entire image sensor on a full-frame camera, while **EF-S lenses** are designed for crop-sensor DSLRs, such as the Canon Rebel series. When mounted on the R50, which has an APS-C sensor, these lenses will perform similarly to how they would on a DSLR crop sensor, providing a "crop factor" effect that extends the effective focal length.

Using Mount Adapters with the Canon EOS R50

1. **Canon Mount Adapter EF-EOS R**

    - The **Canon Mount Adapter EF-EOS R** is a simple, reliable solution for using EF and EF-S lenses with the EOS R50. This adapter allows the camera and lens to communicate electronically, preserving features like autofocus, image stabilization, and lens metadata.

    - The adapter does not alter the optical performance of the lenses but extends the flange distance, enabling compatibility between the older EF/EF-S lenses and the RF mount.

2. **Control Ring Mount Adapter EF-EOS R**

    - The **Control Ring Mount Adapter EF-EOS R** is a step up from the standard adapter and adds a customizable **control ring**. This ring can be programmed to adjust settings like **aperture, ISO, or exposure compensation** directly from the adapter, giving you more control without needing to access the camera menu.

    - This control ring provides an added convenience for professionals who want to adjust settings on the fly, making it a popular choice for photographers who value intuitive, hands-on adjustments.

3. **Drop-In Filter Mount Adapter EF-EOS R**

    - The **Drop-In Filter Mount Adapter EF-EOS R** offers a unique feature: the ability to use **drop-in filters** directly in the adapter. This option is ideal if you're using wide-angle lenses or lenses without filter threads, as the drop-in design allows you to add neutral density (ND) or polarizing filters.

- This adapter is beneficial for landscape photographers who frequently use ND or polarizing filters to control light and reflections. Rather than attaching filters to each lens, this adapter allows you to change filters quickly when switching lenses.

Choosing the Right Lenses for Different Photography Styles

1. **Portrait Photography**

    - For portraits, lenses with **shallow depth of field** and good background blur (bokeh) are ideal. RF prime lenses, such as the **RF 50mm f/1.8** or the **RF 85mm f/2**, are popular choices because they offer sharp detail and smooth background blur, helping the subject stand out.

    - If you have an EF lens collection, using an adapter to attach the **EF 85mm f/1.8** or similar portrait lenses can also work effectively for portrait photography on the EOS R50.

2. **Landscape Photography**

    - For wide-angle shots, lenses such as the **RF 15-35mm f/2.8L** provide a broader field of view, perfect for capturing expansive landscapes.

    - Using an adapter, EF lenses like the **EF 16-35mm f/4L IS** can be equally effective for landscape shots. The use of adapters is especially handy for landscape photographers who may already own a collection of EF wide-angle lenses.

3. **Wildlife and Sports Photography**

    - Telephoto lenses are essential for wildlife and sports to capture distant subjects. Lenses like the **RF 100-500mm f/4.5-7.1L IS USM** offer a long reach, enabling you to shoot close-up details even from afar.

    - For those with an EF lens collection, telephoto lenses such as the **EF 70-200mm f/2.8L IS** paired with an adapter can serve the same purpose, delivering high-quality, distant shots with powerful image stabilization.

4. **Macro Photography**

    - The **RF 35mm f/1.8 Macro IS STM** is a popular macro lens for the EOS R50, allowing you to capture small details with high precision.

- If you already own an EF macro lens, such as the **EF 100mm f/2.8L Macro IS**, using an adapter will enable you to achieve similar close-up shots on the EOS R50 with minimal loss in performance.

Step-by-Step Guide to Using Lens Adapters with the Canon EOS R50

Step 1: Attach the Lens Adapter to the Camera

- Begin by aligning the **red alignment dot** on the adapter with the corresponding dot on the camera body.
- Rotate the adapter clockwise until you feel it click securely into place. This indicates the adapter is properly attached.

Step 2: Attach the EF or EF-S Lens to the Adapter

- Align the **red (EF) or white (EF-S)** dot on the lens with the alignment dot on the adapter.
- Rotate the lens until it clicks into place. Now, the lens is securely attached to the camera via the adapter.

Step 3: Adjust Settings for Optimal Performance

- **Select Appropriate Focus Mode**:

  Switch to **One-Shot AF** for still subjects or **AI Servo AF** for moving subjects. The adapter maintains compatibility with Canon's AF modes, allowing for continuous autofocus tracking.

- **Use Stabilization Settings**:

  If the lens or camera offers image stabilization, enable it for handheld shots. Stabilization will help counteract any minor hand movements that could blur your images, especially with telephoto lenses.

Step 4: Test for Desired Image Quality

- Check for **sharpness, color balance, and distortion** when using EF or EF-S lenses. While the adapter typically maintains the lens's optical quality, testing a few shots can help ensure that the setup meets your standards.
- If using the **Control Ring Adapter**, experiment with the control ring to see which setting adjustments (ISO, aperture, or exposure) feel most intuitive for your shooting style.

Practical Tips for Working with Lens Adapters

1. **Check Compatibility**: While most EF and EF-S lenses work seamlessly with adapters, some third-party lenses might not be fully compatible. Ensure that your lens is on Canon's list of compatible lenses to avoid issues.

2. **Balance and Stability**: Some EF and EF-S lenses, especially long telephoto lenses, can be heavier than the EOS R50 body. Consider using a **tripod** for added stability or invest in a **tripod collar** for telephoto lenses to prevent strain on the camera mount.

3. **Focus Peaking for Manual Focus**: If you're using manual focus on adapted lenses, enable **focus peaking** on the EOS R50. This feature highlights the in-focus areas of your subject, making manual focus easier to achieve.

4. **Experiment with Drop-In Filters**: If you often work with ND or polarizing filters, the Drop-In Filter Mount Adapter can be incredibly convenient. This setup allows you to change filters without detaching the lens, making it ideal for quick adjustments in the field.

Conclusion

The Canon EOS R50 offers a world of possibilities when paired with the right lenses. While RF lenses are designed to maximize the performance of mirrorless cameras, EF and EF-S lenses can also be used with adapters, expanding your lens choices. With a clear understanding of compatibility and the proper use of adapters, you can explore a wide variety of photography styles—from close-up macro shots to far-reaching wildlife captures—all with your EOS R50. Whether you're a beginner looking to get started or a professional exploring new creative options, mastering lens compatibility and adapter use will enhance your Canon experience and elevate your photography results.

Using Lens Filters and Other Accessories

Lens filters and accessories are essential tools for any photographer, enhancing your ability to create specific effects, improve image quality, and protect your equipment. For Canon EOS R50 users, understanding how to select and use these accessories can elevate your photography from good to extraordinary. This section explains various types of lens filters, how to choose the right ones for different shooting conditions, and introduces other essential accessories like lens hoods, cleaning tools, and more.

The Basics of Lens Filters for the Canon EOS R50

Lens filters are pieces of glass or resin that attach to the front of your lens, allowing you to control light, color, and contrast before it reaches the camera sensor. While you can often make adjustments in post-processing, using filters on the camera helps capture the desired effects straight from the camera. Filters come in a variety of types, each suited for a specific purpose.

1. **UV and Protective Filters**

UV (Ultraviolet) filters were initially designed to block ultraviolet light, which could create a hazy effect in images when shooting film photography. In digital photography, UV light doesn't usually affect image quality. However, UV filters remain popular as **protective filters** because they create a barrier between your lens and the outside environment.

Using UV Filters on the EOS R50:

- A UV filter is particularly useful for photographers who shoot outdoors or in unpredictable conditions. If you're photographing near sand, water, or in busy settings, a UV filter provides a layer of protection for your lens, keeping it safe from scratches, dust, and fingerprints.
- Since UV filters are usually clear, they don't affect the exposure or color of your images, making them a safe option to leave on your lens all the time.

2. **Polarizing Filters**

Polarizing filters are an excellent choice for outdoor photography, as they reduce reflections and glare while boosting color contrast and saturation.

Polarizing filters work by filtering out light waves that are scattered in different directions, which helps to cut through reflections on non-metallic surfaces like water, glass, and wet leaves.

Using Polarizing Filters on the EOS R50:

- To attach a polarizing filter, simply screw it onto the front of your lens. Many polarizers are **circular polarizers,** which allow you to rotate the filter to achieve the desired effect.
- Rotate the filter while looking through the viewfinder until you see reduced reflections or enhanced colors. Polarizing filters are especially useful for landscape photography, bringing out the blues in the sky and the greens in foliage.

3. **Neutral Density (ND) Filters**

Neutral Density (ND) filters reduce the amount of light entering the lens without affecting color balance. These filters are essentially "sunglasses" for your camera, allowing you to use slower shutter speeds or wider apertures even in bright conditions.

ND filters come in various "stops," indicating how much light they block. A 3-stop ND filter, for example, reduces light by 3 stops, while a 10-stop filter drastically cuts light, allowing for long exposures even in daylight.

Using ND Filters on the EOS R50:

- ND filters are ideal for creating smooth, flowing water effects, capturing motion blur in clouds, or reducing the light when you want a shallower depth of field in bright light.
- To use an ND filter, select the desired stop value for your effect, attach the filter to your lens, and then adjust your settings on the EOS R50 to match your creative goals. For instance, if you're capturing a waterfall, a 6-stop ND filter may allow you to use a slower shutter speed to create a silky water effect.

4. **Graduated ND Filters**

Graduated ND filters are similar to regular ND filters but with a gradual transition from dark to clear. They are useful for scenes where the sky is much brighter than the landscape, allowing you to balance the exposure between the two.

Using Graduated ND Filters on the EOS R50:

- Graduated ND filters come in both hard and soft transitions. Hard-edge filters have an abrupt line between dark and clear, while soft-edge filters have a gradual transition.
- To use a graduated ND filter, position the darker section over the brighter area of the scene, such as the sky, to reduce its brightness and bring balance to the exposure. This technique is particularly effective for sunrise or sunset shots.

5. **Color Filters**

Color filters are used to adjust or emphasize colors in your photos. They are more commonly used in black-and-white photography to control contrast or in specific color-corrective situations.

Using Color Filters on the EOS R50:

- For black-and-white photography, red filters can make skies appear darker and add dramatic contrast, while yellow filters enhance skin tones. Green filters can lighten foliage for a brighter landscape effect.
- In digital photography, color filters are less essential, as white balance and color adjustments can be made in post-processing. However, they can still provide unique effects for those seeking a particular aesthetic.

Other Essential Accessories for the Canon EOS R50

1. **Lens Hoods**

Lens hoods are accessories that fit onto the front of the lens, extending slightly past the edge. They help to block stray light from hitting the lens, reducing lens flare and enhancing contrast in bright conditions.

Using Lens Hoods on the EOS R50:

- Each lens typically has a specific lens hood model designed for it, so choose one compatible with your lens's focal length. For example, wide-angle lenses have shorter lens hoods, while telephoto lenses have longer ones.

- Attach the lens hood by aligning it with the markings on the lens and twisting it until it clicks into place. Lens hoods are beneficial for outdoor and backlit photography, where light sources can create unwanted reflections.

2. **Cleaning Accessories**

Keeping your lens and camera clean is essential for capturing sharp, clear images. **Cleaning accessories** such as a microfiber cloth, lens cleaning solution, and an air blower can help maintain your equipment.

Using Cleaning Accessories on the EOS R50:

- Use an air blower to remove loose dust and debris from your lens and camera body.

- For smudges or fingerprints on your lens, gently wipe the glass with a microfiber cloth and, if necessary, apply a small amount of lens cleaning solution to the cloth.

- Regular cleaning helps prevent scratches and keeps your lens performing at its best.

3. **Lens Cap and Rear Cap**

Lens caps protect the front glass element of your lens, while **rear caps** protect the lens's rear element when it's not attached to the camera.

Using Lens and Rear Caps on the EOS R50:

- Always cover your lens with the cap when it's not in use to avoid dust, smudges, and scratches.

- Ensure the rear cap is securely in place when storing lenses separately to protect the lens mount and rear glass element.

4. **Camera Strap**

A **camera strap** can make a big difference, especially for handheld shooting. Canon provides a strap with the EOS R50, but you might want to invest in a padded or quick-release strap for extra comfort.

Using a Camera Strap on the EOS R50:

- Attach the strap to the designated loops on either side of the camera body. If using a quick-release strap, ensure it's securely fastened.

- Straps are helpful for steadying your camera while shooting and provide security when you're on the move.

5. **Remote Shutter Release**

A **remote shutter release** allows you to trigger the camera without physically touching it, which is especially useful for long exposures, self-portraits, or situations where camera shake would affect the image.

Using a Remote Shutter Release on the EOS R50:

- Attach the remote shutter release via the camera's compatible port, or connect a wireless remote if available.

- Once connected, press the remote button to take a photo, reducing the chances of blur caused by pressing the shutter manually.

6. **Tripods**

A **tripod** is one of the most important accessories for any photographer, especially for low-light, landscape, and long-exposure photography. It provides stability, allowing for sharp images at slow shutter speeds.

Using a Tripod with the EOS R50:

- Mount the camera onto the tripod's quick-release plate and securely attach it to the tripod head.

- Adjust the tripod legs to the desired height and lock them in place. For added stability, especially in windy conditions, consider using a weight or sandbag attached to the tripod's center column.

7. **Battery Grip**

A **battery grip** can extend the battery life and improve handling, particularly useful for longer shooting sessions.

Using a Battery Grip on the EOS R50:

- Attach the battery grip to the camera's battery compartment, securing it firmly.
- Battery grips provide additional power and a better grip for vertical shooting, especially useful for portrait photographers or those on extended shoots.

8. **Memory Cards and Card Readers**

Fast, reliable **memory cards** are essential for storing and transferring images. Choosing the right card speed and capacity ensures smooth performance.

Using Memory Cards with the EOS R50:

- Insert the memory card into the camera's card slot, following the alignment guide.
- Consider using a card reader for faster file transfers when moving photos to a computer.

Conclusion

Using the right lens filters and accessories can significantly enhance your Canon EOS R50 photography experience. From UV filters that protect your lens to ND and polarizing filters that transform your photos, each accessory serves a unique purpose. When combined with additional essentials like tripods, remote shutters, and lens hoods, these tools provide stability, creativity, and versatility. Experimenting with these filters and accessories will allow you to create images with greater depth, detail, and professionalism.

Working with External Flashes and Tripods

When it comes to maximizing the potential of the Canon EOS R50, understanding how to effectively use external flashes and tripods is essential for both beginners and professionals. These accessories significantly enhance your ability to capture high-quality images, whether you are working in low light, shooting portraits, or aiming for stability in long exposure photography. This chapter will break down the basics of working with these accessories, explain how they function, and provide step-by-step guidance for their practical use.

External Flashes: Enhancing Lighting

External flashes are a crucial tool for photographers who need more control over lighting conditions than what the built-in camera flash can offer. While the Canon EOS R50 comes equipped with a capable built-in flash, an external flash provides greater flexibility, more power, and a variety of creative options.

Why Use an External Flash? An external flash can make a dramatic difference in your photography by:

- **Providing More Power**: External flashes have a higher light output than the built-in camera flash, allowing you to illuminate larger areas or subjects.

- **Offering Directional Lighting**: Unlike built-in flashes, external flashes can be tilted or rotated to bounce light off ceilings or walls, creating softer and more natural-looking lighting.

- **Reducing Red-Eye**: The position of an external flash is farther from the camera lens, which helps to minimize the common red-eye effect in portraits.

- **Allowing Advanced Features**: Many external flashes come with features such as TTL (Through-The-Lens) metering, which automatically adjusts flash output based on the scene, and high-speed sync for shooting at faster shutter speeds.

Types of External Flashes There are various types of external flashes that can be used with the Canon EOS R50:

- **Speedlites**: These are compact, portable flashes that can be mounted on the camera's hot shoe. Canon's Speedlite series, such as the Speedlite EL-100, offers great compatibility with the EOS R50.

- **Studio Strobes**: Larger, more powerful flashes that are often used in studio settings. They require additional equipment like stands and power sources but are ideal for professional setups.

- **Ring Flashes**: Special flashes that create uniform light around the subject, often used in macro photography and portrait work.

Setting Up and Using an External Flash

- **Mount the Flash**: Slide the external flash onto the camera's hot shoe and secure it in place by locking it down.
- **Adjust Flash Settings**: Power on the flash and set it to either TTL mode for automatic control or manual mode if you want to adjust the flash output manually.
- **Angle and Position**: Tilt the flash head to bounce the light off a ceiling or wall for softer illumination. Avoid aiming it directly at the subject, as this can create harsh shadows.
- **Test and Adjust**: Take a few test shots and adjust the flash settings or angle as needed to achieve the desired effect.

Tips for Using External Flashes

- **Use Diffusers**: Attaching a diffuser to your flash helps to spread the light evenly, making it softer and more flattering.

- **Understand Flash Compensation**: Use the flash compensation setting on the Canon EOS R50 to increase or decrease the flash output based on the lighting conditions.
- **Experiment with Off-Camera Flash**: For more creative control, use an off-camera flash setup with a wireless trigger to position the light source independently from the camera.

Tripods: Stability and Precision

A tripod is one of the most essential accessories for photographers, whether shooting landscapes, portraits, or long exposure scenes. The Canon EOS R50, like any high-resolution camera, benefits greatly from the stability that a tripod offers.

Why Use a Tripod? Using a tripod can enhance your photography by:

- **Reducing Camera Shake**: Even slight hand movements can cause blur, especially in low-light or long exposure photography. A tripod provides a stable platform that eliminates this issue.
- **Enabling Long Exposures**: For night photography, light painting, or capturing motion blur (e.g., waterfalls or traffic trails), a tripod is essential.
- **Assisting in Composition**: With a tripod, you can carefully frame your shot, make precise adjustments, and keep the camera steady while you take your time composing.
- **Supporting Heavy Lenses**: Some telephoto or macro lenses can be heavy and difficult to hold steady; a tripod helps distribute the weight and provides stability.

Choosing the Right Tripod Selecting the right tripod for your Canon EOS R50 involves understanding the different types available:

- **Compact Tripods**: Lightweight and portable, ideal for travel photography.
- **Full-Size Tripods**: Sturdy and extendable, suitable for studio or outdoor use where more stability is required.
- **Specialty Tripods**: Such as tabletop tripods for low-angle shots or flexible tripods that can be wrapped around poles and branches.

When choosing a tripod, consider the following:

- **Load Capacity**: Ensure the tripod can support the weight of the EOS R50 plus any additional accessories.
- **Material**: Aluminum tripods are budget-friendly but heavier; carbon fiber tripods are lighter and more expensive but provide excellent stability.
- **Height and Portability**: Look for a tripod that can extend to a comfortable shooting height while still being compact enough to carry.

Setting Up and Using a Tripod

- **Extend the Legs**: Spread the tripod legs to provide a wide base, ensuring the camera is stable. Adjust the leg locks or twist mechanisms to set the height.
- **Attach the Camera**: Use the quick-release plate or mounting screw to secure the Canon EOS R50 to the tripod head.
- **Level the Camera**: Use the built-in spirit level or the camera's electronic level (if available) to ensure the camera is perfectly horizontal.
- **Adjust the Tripod Head**: Pan, tilt, or swivel the head to achieve the desired composition. A ball head provides flexible movement, while a three-way head allows for precise adjustments.

Tips for Tripod Use

- **Use a Remote Shutter or Timer**: To avoid camera shake when pressing the shutter button, use a remote control or set a timer on the EOS R50.
- **Stabilize Further**: For added stability, hang a weight from the tripod's center column if it has a hook.
- **Work on Uneven Terrain**: Adjust the tripod legs individually to maintain a level camera on slopes or rough surfaces.

Combining External Flashes and Tripods For more complex photography projects, such as portraits or staged scenes, using both an external flash and a tripod simultaneously can greatly enhance your results. A tripod ensures the camera remains steady while the external flash provides the desired lighting effect. This combination is perfect for:

- **Portrait Photography**: Use the tripod for stability while directing the external flash to bounce light for a soft, even glow.
- **Product Photography**: Position the camera on a tripod and use multiple flashes or continuous lights to create a professional setup.
- **Night Photography**: Capture clear, detailed shots using long exposure on a tripod while illuminating specific areas with an external flash.

Conclusion

By mastering the use of external flashes and tripods with your Canon EOS R50, you can take your photography to the next level. Whether you are a beginner just getting started or a professional looking to refine your skills, understanding these tools will empower you to capture sharper, more beautifully lit images.

CHAPTER 8

VIDEO RECORDING WITH THE CANON EOS R50

Video Settings and Frame Rates

Understanding video settings and frame rates is crucial for anyone looking to make the most out of the Canon EOS R50's video capabilities. Whether you're a beginner aiming to capture simple videos or a professional seeking high-quality footage, mastering these concepts will elevate your videography skills.

The Basics of Video Settings

The Canon EOS R50 offers a variety of video settings that determine the quality, look, and style of your recordings. These settings can affect aspects such as resolution, frame rate, and file format. Here's an overview of essential video settings:

1. Resolution Resolution refers to the number of pixels in each frame of your video. The higher the resolution, the more detail your footage will contain. The Canon EOS R50 supports the following resolutions:

- **4K (3840 x 2160 pixels)**: Ideal for high-quality, professional videos with sharp details. Keep in mind that shooting in 4K can result in larger file sizes and requires more processing power.

- **Full HD (1920 x 1080 pixels)**: A balanced option that provides good quality while keeping file sizes manageable. It's perfect for social media content and most online platforms.

- **HD (1280 x 720 pixels)**: Useful for lower storage needs and faster editing processes, though the quality is less impressive compared to 4K and Full HD.

2. Frame Rate Frame rate refers to the number of individual frames captured per second (fps). The frame rate you choose can impact the overall feel and motion quality of your video. The Canon EOS R50 supports several frame rates:

- **24 fps**: This frame rate is commonly used in cinema and creates a film-like quality. It's ideal for storytelling and projects where a natural motion blur is desirable.

- **30 fps**: A standard frame rate for online videos and television. It delivers smooth and consistent motion and is perfect for most general-purpose recordings.

- **60 fps**: Provides smoother motion, making it a great choice for action-packed scenes or videos requiring slow-motion effects. It's also useful for sports and fast-paced activities.

- **120 fps** (in Full HD or HD): This high frame rate allows for dramatic slow-motion playback when edited down to 24 or 30 fps. It's an excellent option for highlighting details in movement.

Choosing the Right Frame Rate

Choosing the right frame rate depends on the type of video you want to create:

- **24 fps**: Best for narrative and documentary-style videos where a cinematic feel is needed.
- **30 fps**: A versatile option for vlogs, tutorials, and other casual video content.
- **60 fps and above**: Ideal for action scenes, sports, or when creating slow-motion effects. Higher frame rates allow you to slow down footage in post-production, providing a dramatic and detailed result.

Note: Keep in mind that higher frame rates use more storage space and can require more processing power during editing.

Configuring Video Settings on the Canon EOS R50

To set up video recording on the Canon EOS R50, follow these steps:

- **Access the Video Mode**:

    Turn the mode dial to the movie icon to enable video recording mode.

- **Adjust the Resolution and Frame Rate**:

    o Press the "Menu" button and navigate to the video settings tab.

    o Select "Movie Rec Quality" to choose your desired resolution and frame rate.

- **Consider Bit Rate and Compression**:

    Higher bit rates produce better quality but result in larger file sizes. The EOS R50 offers options such as IPB (compressed) and IPB Lite (more compression).

Practical Tips for Choosing Video Settings

1. Match the Frame Rate to Your Subject:

- For interviews or talking-head videos, 24 or 30 fps provides a natural appearance.
- For action or sports, use 60 fps or higher to ensure smooth motion.

2. Use 4K Sparingly:

While 4K provides exceptional quality, it's best reserved for projects where high detail is crucial, as it requires significant storage and editing power.

3. Experiment with Slow Motion:

Use 120 fps for clips where you plan to apply slow-motion effects in post-production. This can add a dramatic flair to action scenes or emphasize specific moments.

Common Issues and How to Avoid Them

- **File Size Management**:

Recording at higher resolutions and frame rates will produce large video files. Make sure your SD card has ample storage and that your computer can handle the file sizes for editing.

- **Overheating Concerns**:

Prolonged recording in 4K or high frame rates can cause the camera to overheat. Keep recording sessions short or take breaks between takes.

- **Compatibility and Editing**:

Ensure your editing software supports the resolution and frame rate you choose. Shooting in 4K might require a more powerful computer for smooth editing.

Conclusion

Mastering the video settings and frame rates on your Canon EOS R50 will greatly enhance your ability to produce professional-level video content. By understanding these fundamentals, you can tailor your settings to match your specific creative needs and achieve outstanding results.

Audio Recording: Internal and External Microphones

Capturing high-quality audio is just as important as recording great video when working with the Canon EOS R50. Understanding how to effectively use both the internal and external microphone options can make a significant difference in the overall quality of your video projects. In this section, we will explore the capabilities of the built-in microphone, the advantages of using external microphones, and step-by-step guidance on how to set them up.

Internal Microphone: Convenience and Limitations

The Canon EOS R50 is equipped with an internal microphone that provides a straightforward way to capture audio without needing any additional equipment. This built-in microphone is useful for:

- **Quick Recording**: Ideal for spontaneous video shoots or when you need to capture sound without carrying extra gear.

- **Basic Audio Needs**: Sufficient for casual vlogs, tutorials, or home videos.

Limitations of the Internal Microphone:

- **Ambient Noise**: The internal microphone tends to pick up background sounds, which can reduce the clarity of your main audio.

- **Limited Sound Range**: It may not capture subtle audio details effectively, making it less ideal for professional-level projects.

- **Lack of Directional Control**: The built-in microphone captures sound from all directions (omnidirectional), which can make it difficult to isolate the desired audio source.

External Microphones: Enhancing Audio Quality

For higher-quality audio, the Canon EOS R50 supports the use of external microphones, which provide superior sound recording and flexibility. Here are some common types of external microphones and their benefits:

1. Shotgun Microphones These are highly directional microphones that capture sound from the front while minimizing noise from the sides and rear.

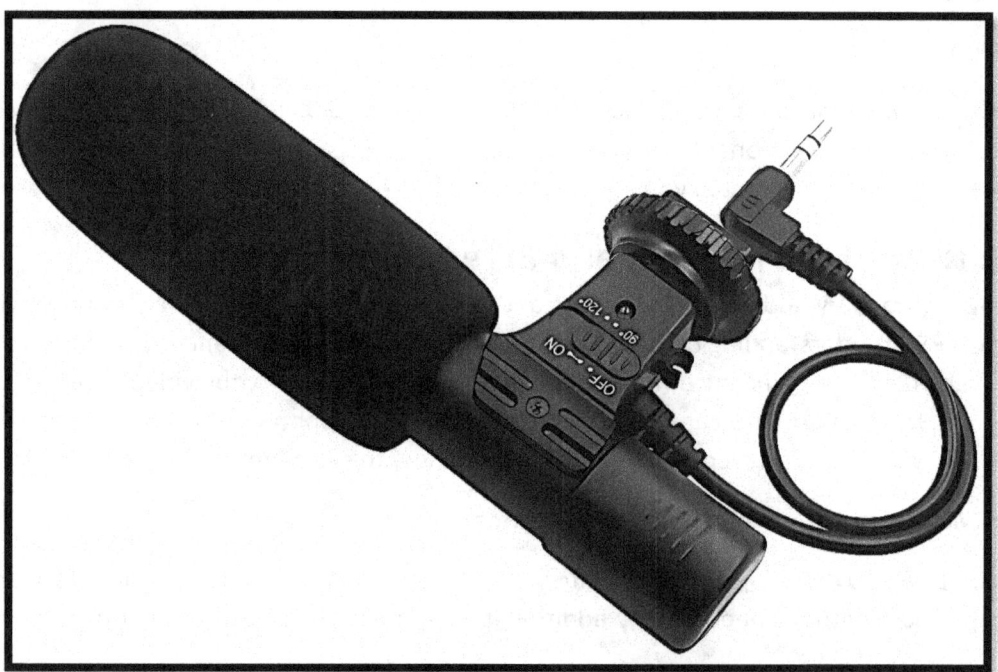

- **Ideal for Interviews and Vlogs**: Shotgun microphones can be mounted on the camera and are perfect for scenarios where you need clear voice recordings.

- **Noise Reduction**: By focusing on the subject, shotgun microphones help reduce unwanted background noise.

2. Lavalier Microphones (Lapels) These small, clip-on microphones are often used for interviews or presentations.

- **Hands-Free Operation**: The microphone can be clipped to a person's clothing, allowing for natural movement.

- **Proximity to Sound Source**: Because they are close to the speaker's mouth, lavalier mics provide clear and consistent audio.

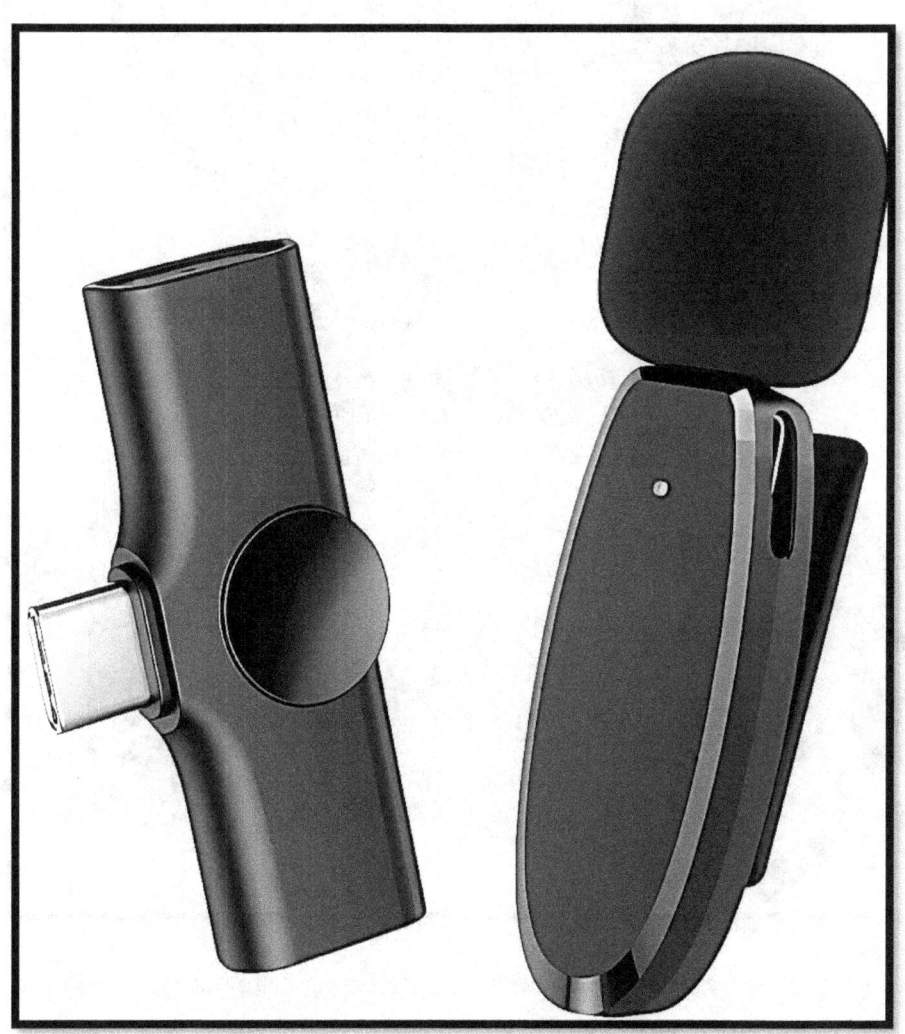

3. Handheld Microphones Handheld mics are versatile and can be used in a variety of settings, from interviews to live presentations.

- **Control and Flexibility**: The user has direct control over the microphone placement.
- **Professional Sound**: Often used in broadcast settings for reliable and high-quality sound.

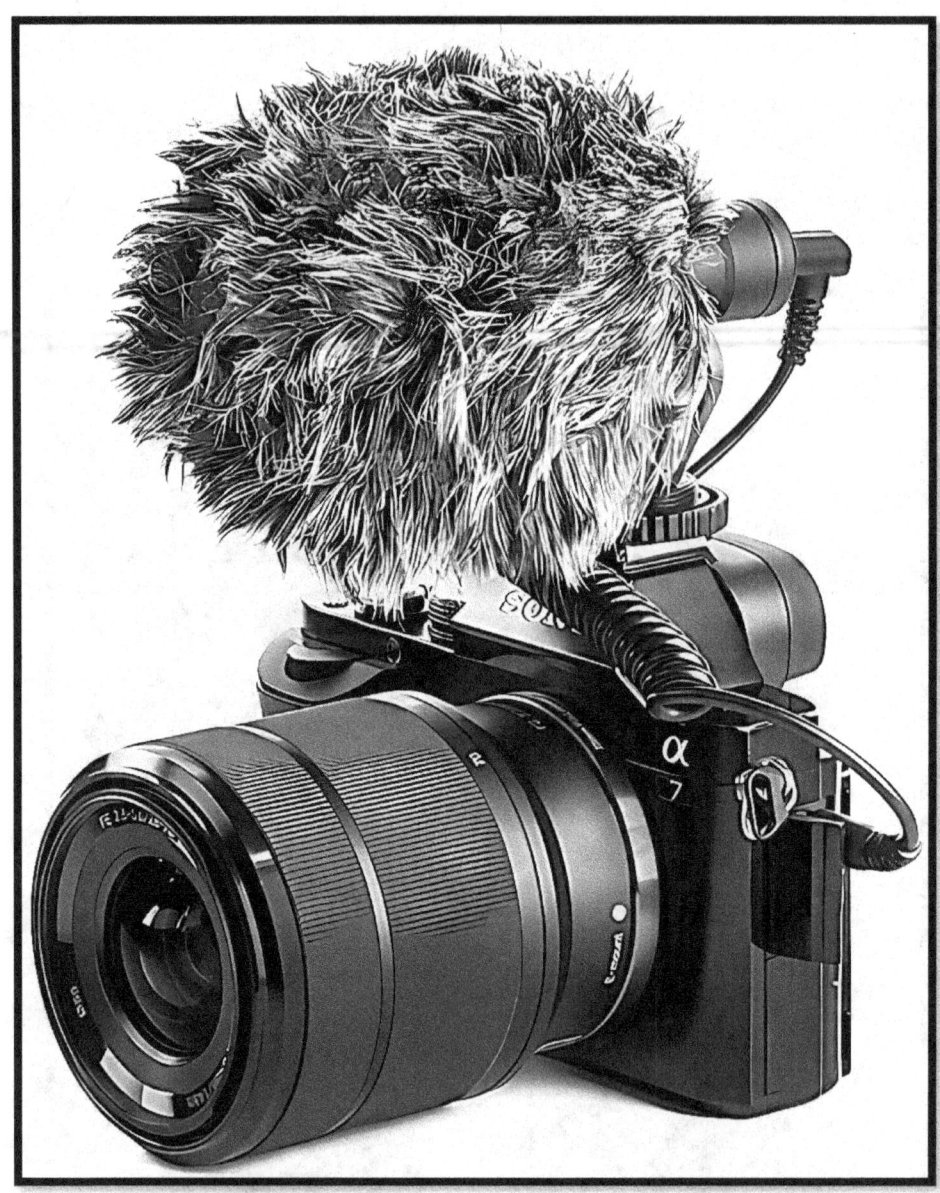

4. Wireless Microphone Systems Wireless setups are excellent for situations where mobility is important.

- **Freedom of Movement**: Wireless mics allow subjects to move freely without being tethered to the camera.
- **Clear Audio**: High-quality wireless systems provide audio clarity comparable to wired systems.

Setting Up an External Microphone with the Canon EOS R50

Using an external microphone with the Canon EOS R50 is simple and can greatly enhance your audio quality. Here's a step-by-step guide:

- **Choose the Right Microphone**: Depending on your project, select a microphone type that suits your needs (e.g., shotgun for vlogs, lavalier for interviews).
- **Connect the Microphone**: Plug the external microphone into the 3.5mm audio input jack on the Canon EOS R50.
- **Secure the Microphone**: For shotgun microphones, use the camera's hot shoe mount for stability. Clip lavalier mics securely to the speaker's clothing.
- **Adjust Audio Settings**: Navigate to the camera's menu, go to the audio settings, and ensure that the external microphone is recognized. Adjust the recording levels to avoid peaking or distortion.
- **Monitor the Audio**: If possible, use headphones connected to the camera or an external monitor to check audio quality during recording.

Tips for Optimizing Audio Quality

- **Position the Microphone Properly**: Always place the microphone as close to the sound source as possible for the clearest audio.
- **Check for Interference**: If using a wireless microphone, ensure that there are no signal interferences that could affect sound quality.
- **Use a Windshield**: For outdoor recordings, use a windscreen or dead cat cover on your microphone to minimize wind noise.
- **Test Before Recording**: Always do a test recording to fine-tune audio levels and detect any issues before starting your main shoot.

Conclusion

Mastering audio recording with both internal and external microphones on the Canon EOS R50 opens up new possibilities for creating professional-quality videos. While the built-in microphone provides a quick solution for basic needs, investing in an external microphone will greatly enhance the sound quality and overall impact of your projects.

Basic Tips for Video Editing

Video editing is an essential skill for anyone looking to create polished and engaging content with their Canon EOS R50. Whether you're a beginner or a professional, understanding how to effectively edit your videos can significantly enhance the final product. In this section, we will discuss some key tips for video editing, including selecting the right software, organizing your footage, basic editing techniques, and adding final touches like music and transitions.

1. Choosing the Right Video Editing Software

The first step to successful video editing is selecting a suitable editing program. There are many options available, from beginner-friendly tools to advanced software.

- **Beginner-Friendly Software**: Applications like iMovie (Mac) and Windows Video Editor are user-friendly and perfect for those new to editing. They provide basic features for trimming, cutting, and adding text.
- **Professional Software**: Programs such as Adobe Premiere Pro, Final Cut Pro, and DaVinci Resolve offer more advanced features for color correction, multi-layer editing, and special effects. While these programs come with a learning curve, they allow for greater creative control.

Tip: If you're just starting out, choose software with a simple interface to avoid feeling overwhelmed. You can always upgrade to more sophisticated programs as your skills improve.

2. Organizing Your Footage

Before you start editing, organize your video clips. This step can save you time and frustration during the editing process.

- **Create Folders**: Sort your footage into folders by date, event, or project. For example, you might have separate folders for raw footage, audio files, and B-roll (supplementary footage).
- **Label Your Clips**: Rename your video clips with descriptive titles such as "Intro_Interview" or "Scene1_B-roll" to make it easier to find specific content.
- **Review Your Footage**: Watch all your clips and take notes on which parts you want to include in your final video. This step helps streamline the editing process and ensures that you use only the best material.

3. Basic Editing Techniques

With your footage organized, it's time to start editing. Here are some fundamental editing techniques to master:

- **Trimming and Cutting**: Remove any unnecessary parts of your video to keep the content concise. Most video editing software allows you to easily cut and trim sections by dragging the ends of the clip.
- **Arranging Clips**: Place your clips on the timeline in the desired order. Experiment with different sequences to find the flow that best tells your story.
- **Splitting Clips**: If you need to insert a B-roll or break up a long scene, use the split tool to divide a clip into multiple sections.

Tip: Keep your edits tight to avoid dragging out scenes unnecessarily. Viewers are more engaged with shorter, well-paced videos.

4. Adding Transitions and Effects

Transitions help make the shift between clips smoother and more visually appealing. However, it's essential to use them sparingly:

- **Simple Transitions**: Basic transitions like fades and cuts often look more professional than over-the-top effects.
- **Consistency**: Use similar transitions throughout your video to maintain a cohesive look.
- **Effects**: Adding color correction or visual effects can enhance your footage, but don't go overboard. Subtle adjustments often yield the best results.

Tip: If your footage has varying lighting conditions, apply color correction to balance the exposure and white balance across clips.

5. Incorporating Audio

Good audio is critical for a professional-looking video. Here's how to optimize it:

- **Background Music**: Add music that complements the mood of your video. Ensure the volume is low enough that it doesn't overpower any dialogue.
- **Audio Levels**: Adjust the levels of your audio tracks to maintain consistent sound. Most video editing software includes audio meters that can help you ensure your sound stays within optimal ranges.
- **Voiceovers**: If needed, record a voiceover using a quality microphone. Position the narration at key points to provide context or emphasize important details.

Tip: Always preview your video with headphones to detect any audio issues that might not be noticeable through standard speakers.

6. Exporting Your Final Video

Once you're satisfied with your edits, it's time to export your video. Follow these steps to ensure the best quality:

- **Choose the Right Format**: MP4 is a common format that balances quality and file size, making it suitable for online uploads.
- **Set the Resolution**: For videos shot on the Canon EOS R50, exporting in 1080p or 4K ensures that you maintain high resolution.
- **Check the Frame Rate**: Export your video at the same frame rate you used during recording to avoid motion inconsistencies.

Tip: Double-check your video's settings and review the final output before sharing it online or saving it to your storage.

Conclusion

Mastering basic video editing techniques can elevate your content from simple clips to professional-quality videos. By choosing the right software, organizing your footage, using effective editing techniques, and paying attention to audio and transitions, you can create videos that engage and impress your audience. With practice, these steps will become second nature, allowing you to take full advantage of your Canon EOS R50's capabilities.

CHAPTER 9

CONNECTIVITY AND IMAGE SHARING

Connecting to Wi-Fi and Bluetooth on the Canon EOS R50

The Canon EOS R50 is equipped with modern connectivity features, including built-in Wi-Fi and Bluetooth, allowing users to transfer images, control the camera remotely, and share content seamlessly. Understanding how to set up and use these connectivity options is essential for both beginners and professionals who want to maximize their workflow and share their work efficiently. In this section, we will guide you through the steps for connecting to Wi-Fi and Bluetooth, explaining each process clearly and providing tips for troubleshooting common issues.

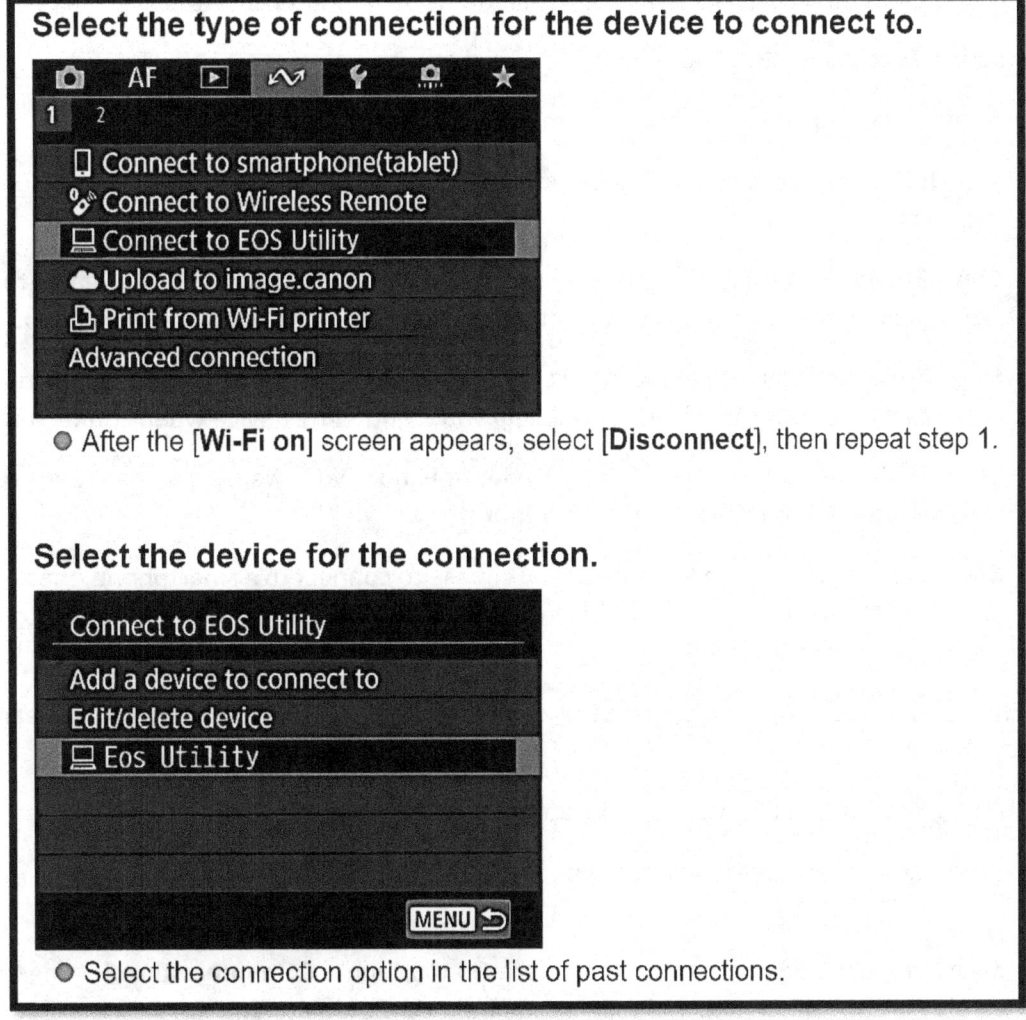

1. Understanding Wi-Fi and Bluetooth on the Canon EOS R50

Before we dive into the step-by-step instructions, it's important to understand what Wi-Fi and Bluetooth can do for your Canon EOS R50.

- **Wi-Fi Connectivity**: This feature allows you to transfer images and videos directly to a computer or mobile device. It also enables remote shooting with a live view on your smartphone or tablet.

- **Bluetooth Connectivity**: Bluetooth maintains a low-power, continuous connection between the camera and a mobile device, making it easier to initiate Wi-Fi connections for image transfer and remote control.

Both Wi-Fi and Bluetooth complement each other; Bluetooth helps establish a quick link to your device, which can then be used to switch to Wi-Fi for more data-intensive tasks.

2. Connecting Your Canon EOS R50 to Wi-Fi

Follow these simple steps to connect your camera to Wi-Fi:

- **Step 1: Turn on the Camera** Ensure your camera is powered on and set to a mode that allows menu access.

- **Step 2: Open the Wi-Fi Settings** Press the Menu button and navigate to the **Communication Settings** under the setup tab. Select **Wi-Fi/Bluetooth Connection**.

- **Step 3: Enable Wi-Fi** Toggle the Wi-Fi setting to **Enable**. You may be prompted to register a nickname for your camera—this will help you identify the device when connecting.

- **Step 4: Select the Function** Choose the function you want, such as **Connect to Smartphone** or **Transfer Images to Computer**.

- **Step 5: Follow On-Screen Prompts** If you choose to connect to a smartphone, the camera will display a QR code. Scan this with your phone to download the Canon Camera Connect app if you haven't already.

Note: Ensure your smartphone or computer is connected to the same Wi-Fi network for seamless pairing.

3. Connecting Your Canon EOS R50 to Bluetooth

Bluetooth connection is simpler and maintains a continuous link between your camera and mobile device.

- **Step 1: Enable Bluetooth on Your Camera** Go to Menu > **Communication Settings** > **Wi-Fi/Bluetooth Connection**, and toggle the Bluetooth setting to **Enable**.

- **Step 2: Pair with Your Smartphone** Open the Canon Camera Connect app on your smartphone and select **Pair with Camera**.

- **Step 3: Complete the Pairing** The camera will search for nearby devices. Select your smartphone from the list, and confirm the pairing code that appears on both devices.

Once paired, Bluetooth will automatically reconnect when both devices are powered on and within range.

4. Benefits and Use Cases

- **Remote Shooting**: Use your smartphone as a remote shutter release for group shots or tricky angles.

- **Instant Image Transfer**: Transfer photos to your phone for quick editing and sharing on social media.

- **Geotagging**: If your smartphone has GPS, Bluetooth can be used to add location data to your images.

5. Troubleshooting Common Issues

- **Connection Fails**: Ensure that both Wi-Fi and Bluetooth are enabled on your camera and mobile device. Restart both devices if necessary.

- **Weak Signal**: Move closer to the Wi-Fi router or make sure there are no physical obstructions.

- **Compatibility Issues**: Ensure the Canon Camera Connect app is up to date and that your smartphone's operating system is compatible.

Tips for a Seamless Experience

- **Keep Firmware Updated**: Regular updates often fix connectivity bugs and improve performance.

- **Use 5GHz Wi-Fi When Possible**: It provides faster transfer speeds compared to 2.4GHz.

- **Charge Your Devices**: Ensure your camera and smartphone are sufficiently charged to prevent interruptions during transfer or remote shooting.

Conclusion

By mastering the Wi-Fi and Bluetooth settings on your Canon EOS R50, you can streamline your workflow and make your photography or videography sessions more efficient and enjoyable.

Remote Shooting with the Canon App

Remote shooting with the Canon EOS R50 and the Canon Camera Connect app opens up a world of creative possibilities and convenience. Whether you want to capture wildlife from a distance, take group photos without being behind the camera, or experiment with new photography angles, the remote shooting feature is an invaluable tool for both beginners and professionals. This section will explain how to set up and use remote shooting effectively, providing clear and straightforward instructions.

1. What is Remote Shooting and Why Use It?

Remote shooting allows you to control your Canon EOS R50 from a smartphone or tablet using the Canon Camera Connect app. This feature provides a live view of what the camera sees, and you can adjust settings, trigger the shutter, and even record video directly from your device.

Benefits of Remote Shooting:

- **Convenience**: Capture photos without physically handling the camera, ideal for group shots or self-portraits.

- **New Perspectives**: Position the camera in hard-to-reach places and control it remotely.

- **Reduced Camera Shake**: Avoid touching the camera for long exposure or macro shots, ensuring sharper images.

2. Setting Up the Canon Camera Connect App

Before you can start remote shooting, you need to download and set up the Canon Camera Connect app.

- **Step 1: Download the App** Download the Canon Camera Connect app from the App Store (iOS) or Google Play Store (Android). Ensure your device's operating system is compatible with the app.

- **Step 2: Turn on the Camera** Power on your Canon EOS R50 and press the Menu button.

- **Step 3: Enable Wi-Fi/Bluetooth** Go to **Communication Settings** and enable Wi-Fi/Bluetooth. Ensure that your camera's Wi-Fi function is set to **Enabled**.

- **Step 4: Select the Connection Type** Choose **Connect to Smartphone** from the Wi-Fi/Bluetooth menu. The camera will display a QR code or network information.

- **Step 5: Pair Your Device** Open the Canon Camera Connect app and follow the prompts to connect. If using Bluetooth, ensure Bluetooth is enabled on your device for a seamless pairing process.

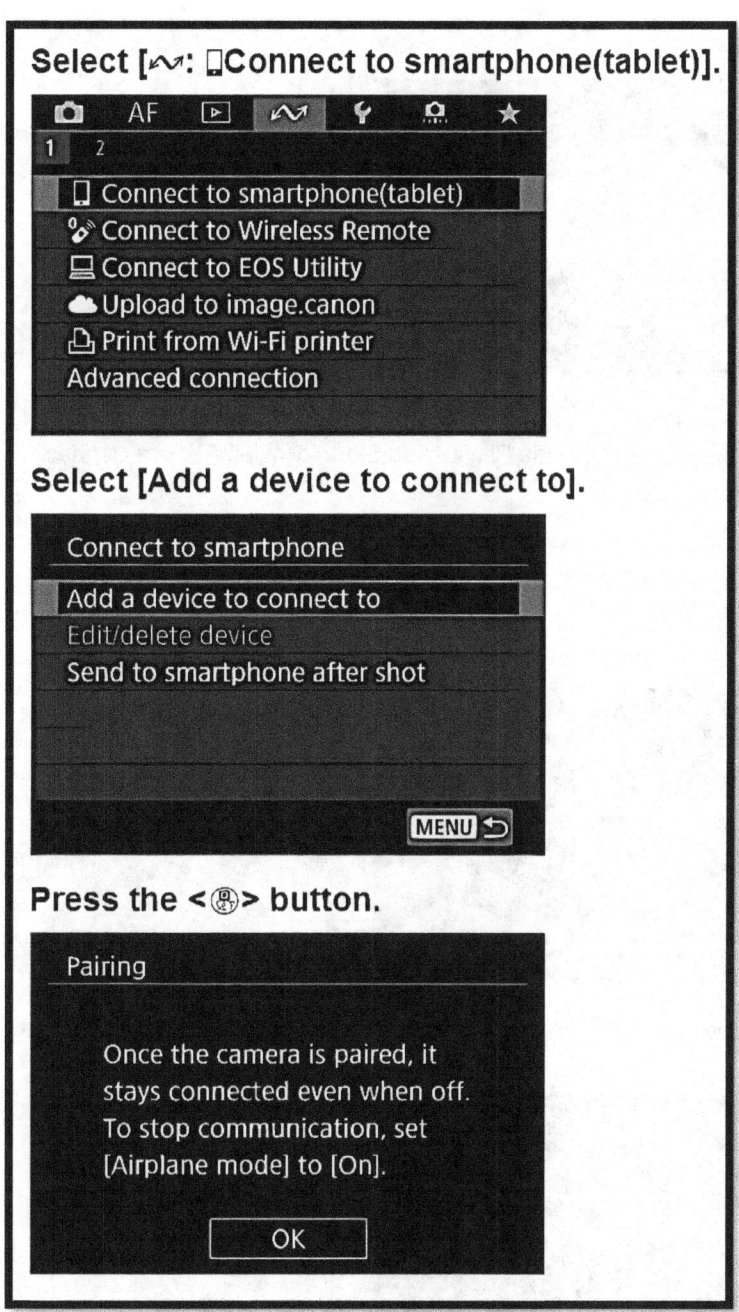

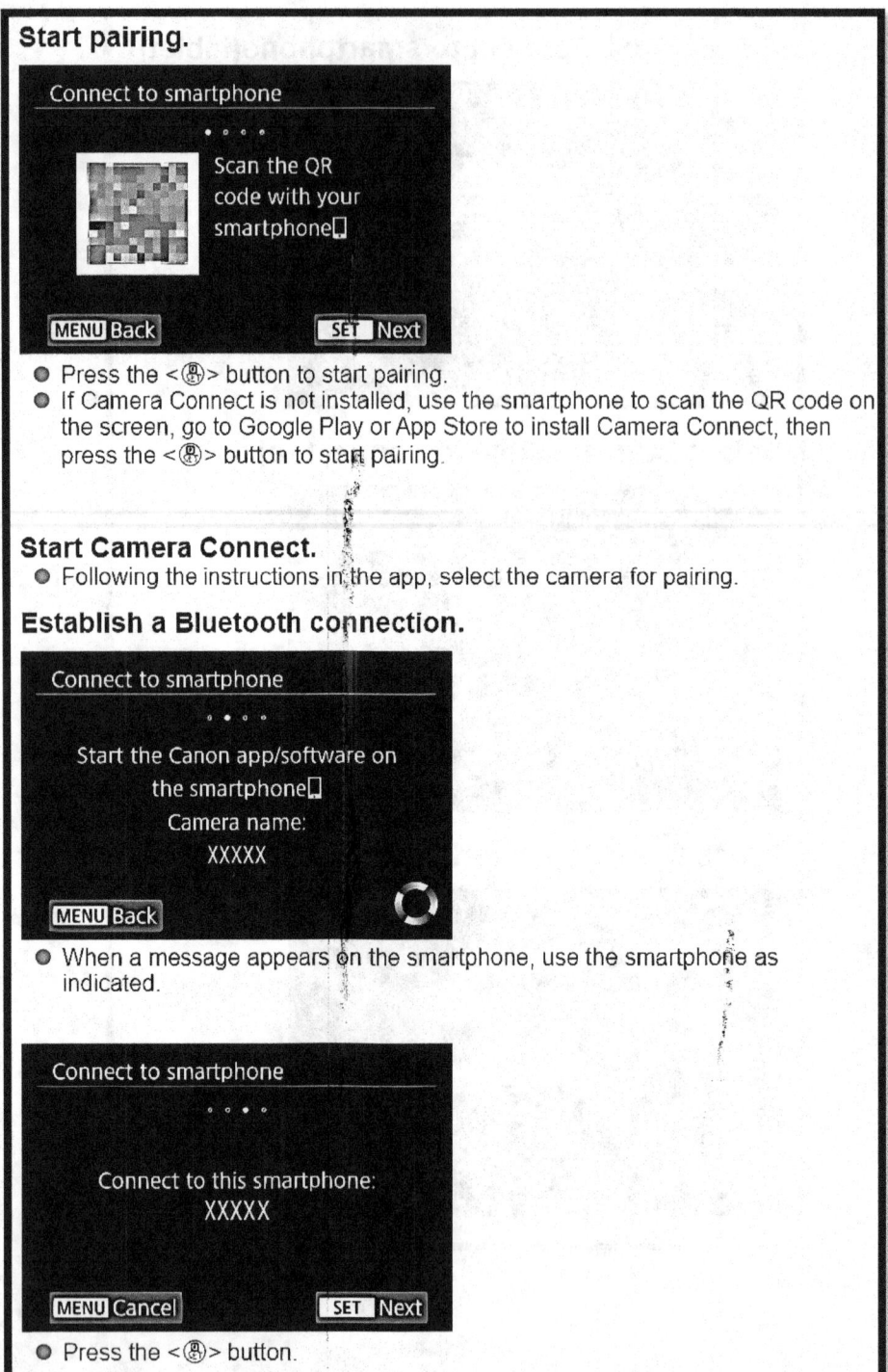

Start pairing.

- Press the <⊛> button to start pairing.
- If Camera Connect is not installed, use the smartphone to scan the QR code on the screen, go to Google Play or App Store to install Camera Connect, then press the <⊛> button to start pairing.

Start Camera Connect.

- Following the instructions in the app, select the camera for pairing.

Establish a Bluetooth connection.

- When a message appears on the smartphone, use the smartphone as indicated.

- Press the <⊛> button.

Complete the pairing process.

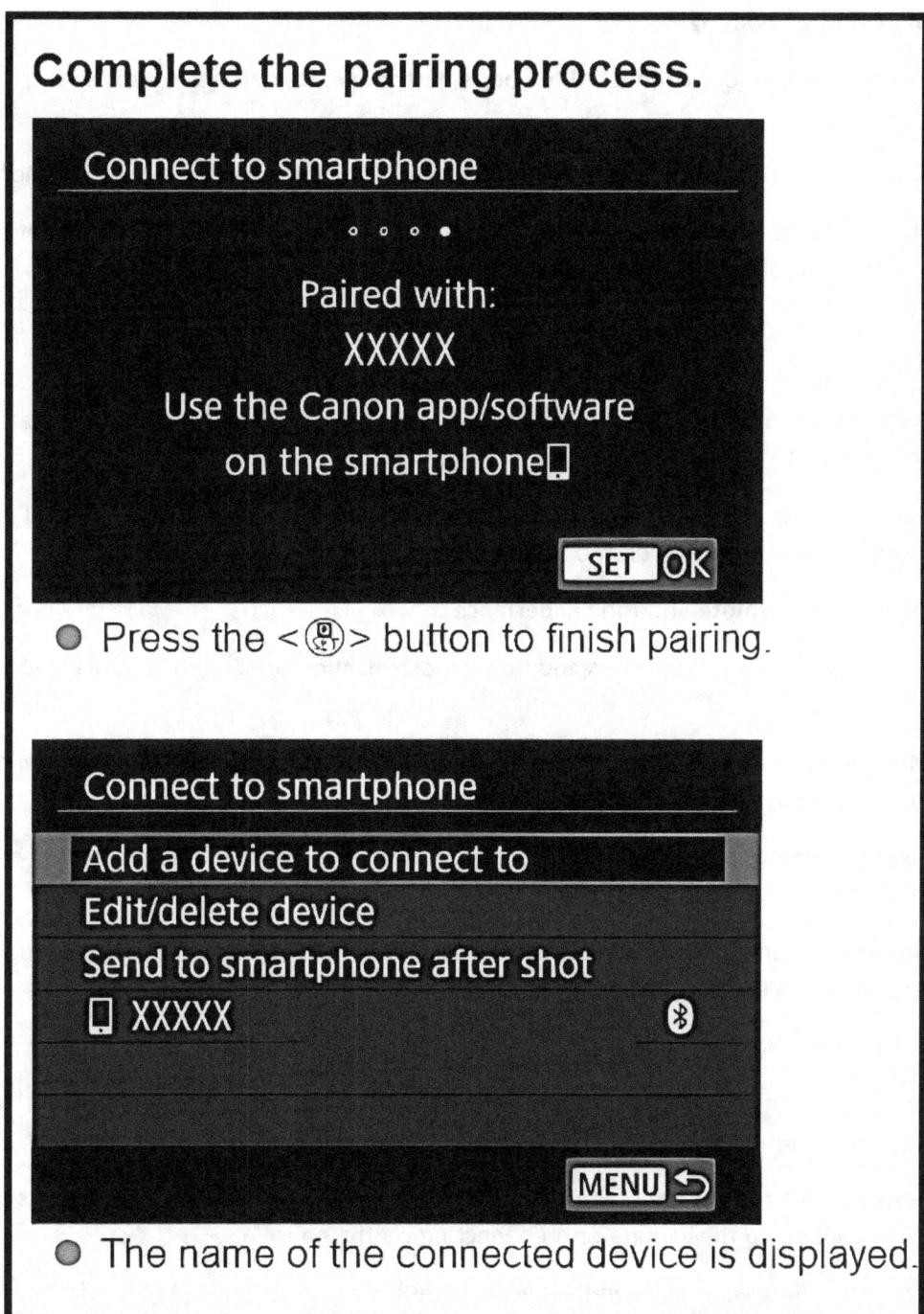

- Press the <⊕> button to finish pairing.

- The name of the connected device is displayed.

3. Initiating Remote Shooting

Once your Canon EOS R50 is connected to your smartphone, follow these steps to start remote shooting:

- **Step 1: Open the Canon Camera Connect App** Launch the app on your smartphone.

- **Step 2: Choose Remote Live View Shooting** Tap on **Remote Live View Shooting**. This option will provide a live feed of what the camera lens is seeing.

- **Step 3: Adjust Camera Settings** Use the app interface to adjust settings such as aperture, shutter speed, ISO, and exposure compensation.

- **Step 4: Compose Your Shot** Frame your subject using the live view on your smartphone. You can tap to focus on specific areas, ensuring accurate focus.

- **Step 5: Capture the Image or Video** Once satisfied with the composition and settings, press the shutter button on the app to take a photo or start video recording.

4. Customizing Your Remote Shooting Experience

The Canon Camera Connect app offers additional customization options to enhance your remote shooting experience:

- **Manual Focus Adjustment**: For precise focusing, switch to manual focus mode and adjust the focus directly from your smartphone.

- **Timer Function**: Set a timer for delayed shooting to capture images at just the right moment.

- **Grid Display and Level**: Activate these tools within the app to ensure your composition is straight and well-balanced.

5. Troubleshooting Common Issues

While remote shooting with the Canon Camera Connect app is generally straightforward, you may encounter a few common issues:

- **Connection Drops**: If the connection between the camera and smartphone is lost, try moving closer to the camera or reconnecting via the app.

- **Slow Live View Feed**: A lag in the live view feed may occur due to Wi-Fi interference or a slow smartphone. Ensure both devices are within range and close unnecessary background apps.

- **App Crashes**: Regularly update the app and your smartphone's operating system to minimize crashes.

6. Tips for Optimal Remote Shooting

To get the most out of remote shooting, follow these best practices:

- **Maintain a Stable Connection**: Stay within a reasonable distance from the camera to prevent interruptions.
- **Use a Tripod**: For stability and sharper images, mount your Canon EOS R50 on a tripod.
- **Monitor Battery Life**: Remote shooting can drain your camera's battery faster. Ensure both your camera and smartphone have sufficient charge before a session.

Conclusion

Remote shooting with the Canon EOS R50 and the Canon Camera Connect app is an essential tool that adds flexibility and creative freedom to your photography. By following these simple steps and tips, you can capture stunning images and videos while enjoying the convenience of remote control.

Transferring Images to Mobile Devices or Computers

Transferring images from your Canon EOS R50 to mobile devices or computers is essential for editing, sharing, or backing up your work. This subtopic covers different methods to achieve seamless image transfer, suitable for both beginners and professionals. Understanding these processes ensures you can quickly and efficiently move your images to your preferred device.

1. Transferring Images to Mobile Devices

The Canon Camera Connect app is a powerful tool that simplifies transferring images to your smartphone or tablet. Here's a detailed guide on how to use it:

Step-by-Step Process Using the Canon Camera Connect App:

- **Connect Your Camera to the App**:
    - Ensure your Canon EOS R50 is powered on and Wi-Fi/Bluetooth is enabled.
    - Open the Canon Camera Connect app on your smartphone or tablet.
    - Select the camera's network name from your device's Wi-Fi settings if not already connected.
- **Select and Transfer Images**:

- Once connected, you will see a live preview of the images stored on your camera.
- Browse through the thumbnails and select the images you want to transfer.
- Tap the **Download** button, and the images will start transferring to your mobile device.

Tips for Mobile Transfers:

- **Use High-Speed Wi-Fi**: For faster image transfers, ensure both your camera and mobile device are connected to a stable and fast Wi-Fi network.
- **Batch Download**: To save time, you can select multiple images to transfer in one go.
- **Image Quality Options**: The app lets you choose between transferring images in their original quality or a smaller size for quicker transfers.

2. Transferring Images to Computers

For photographers who prefer editing and managing their photos on a larger screen, transferring images to a computer is an important step. There are several methods to achieve this:

Method 1: USB Cable Transfer

Using a USB cable is one of the simplest and most reliable methods for transferring images.

- **Connect the Camera to the Computer**: Plug one end of the USB cable into the camera and the other end into a USB port on your computer.
- **Access the Camera's Storage**: Once connected, your computer should recognize the camera as an external storage device. Open the device folder to view your images.
- **Copy and Paste Images**: Select the images or folders you wish to transfer and drag them to your preferred location on your computer.

Method 2: Wi-Fi Transfer Using Canon's Software

Canon provides software like **EOS Utility** to help with wireless transfers.

- **Install EOS Utility**:

    Download and install EOS Utility from Canon's official website.

- **Connect Your Camera to Wi-Fi**:
    - Go to the Wi-Fi/Bluetooth settings on your Canon EOS R50 and choose **Connect to Computer**.

- o   Follow the on-screen instructions to pair the camera with your computer.

- **Transfer Images Using EOS Utility**:

  - o   Open EOS Utility on your computer. The software will automatically detect the connected camera.

  - o   Browse and select the images you want to transfer, and click **Download**.

Tips for Computer Transfers:

- **Ensure the Latest Firmware**: Keeping your camera firmware up to date helps maintain compatibility and transfer efficiency.

- **Use a Stable Wi-Fi Connection**: For wireless transfers, ensure your computer and camera are on the same Wi-Fi network.

3. Transferring Images Using a Memory Card Reader

A memory card reader offers another efficient way to transfer images to your computer, especially when handling a large volume of high-resolution files.

Step-by-Step Process:

- **Remove the Memory Card from the Camera**:

Turn off the camera before removing the memory card.

- **Insert the Memory Card into the Reader**:

Place the memory card into the card reader and connect it to your computer.

- **Access and Transfer Files**:

Open the memory card folder on your computer, select the desired images, and copy them to your chosen folder.

Advantages of Using a Memory Card Reader:

- **Faster Transfer Speeds**: Card readers often provide higher transfer rates compared to USB cable transfers.

- **Direct Access**: Ideal for bulk transfers without draining the camera's battery.

4. Choosing the Right Method for Your Needs

Each transfer method has its own set of advantages, so it's important to choose the one that fits your workflow:

- **For Quick Mobile Transfers**: Use the Canon Camera Connect app.
- **For Secure and Direct Computer Transfers**: A USB cable is reliable.
- **For Large Batches**: A memory card reader is the most efficient option.
- **For Wireless Convenience**: Utilize EOS Utility for cable-free transfers.

Conclusion

By understanding these methods, you can streamline your process and ensure your images are ready for sharing, editing, or backup in no time.

CHAPTER 10

TROUBLESHOOTING AND MAINTENANCE

Common Camera Issues and Solutions

The Canon EOS R50 is a powerful and compact mirrorless camera designed to meet the needs of both beginners and professionals. Like any sophisticated piece of technology, however, it can sometimes encounter issues, from minor inconveniences to occasional technical glitches. Knowing how to troubleshoot these common problems can save you time and ensure your camera is always ready for capturing stunning shots.

In this section, we'll explore some of the most common issues users might face with the Canon EOS R50 and provide step-by-step solutions for each one. We'll also cover preventive tips to help you avoid these issues in the future.

Issue 1: Camera Won't Turn On

One of the most common and frustrating issues with any electronic device is when it fails to power on. For the Canon EOS R50, this can happen for several reasons.

Possible Causes:

- **Battery Drain**: The battery may be drained or improperly installed.
- **Battery Contacts**: Dirt or debris on battery contacts can interfere with proper connection.
- **Power Button**: Sometimes, users may not press the power button firmly enough.

Solution:

- **Check Battery Charge**: Remove the battery and charge it fully. After charging, reinsert it carefully, ensuring the battery compartment door clicks shut.
- **Clean Battery Contacts**: If the camera still doesn't turn on, check the battery contacts for dirt or dust. Use a microfiber cloth to clean them gently.
- **Try Another Battery**: If possible, test a different, fully charged battery. This can rule out issues with the battery itself.
- **Reset Camera Settings**: If the camera was recently updated, it might need a quick reset. Take out the battery, wait 10 seconds, and reinsert it to see if it powers on.

Prevention Tips:

- Regularly check and clean the battery contacts.

- Keep a spare, fully charged battery on hand, especially for extended shoots.

Issue 2: Autofocus Not Working Properly

The Canon EOS R50 offers an impressive autofocus system, but sometimes it might fail to lock onto the subject correctly or focus slowly in certain scenarios.

Possible Causes:

- **Low Light Conditions**: Autofocus systems often struggle in low light.
- **Incorrect Autofocus Mode**: If you're in a mode unsuitable for the subject, such as landscape mode for a moving object, the camera may not focus accurately.
- **Lens Issue**: Sometimes, dirt or debris on the lens or even a loose lens connection can affect autofocus.

Solution:

- **Adjust Autofocus Mode**: Check the current autofocus mode (such as One-Shot AF, Servo AF, etc.). For moving subjects, Servo AF is typically more effective.
- **Increase Lighting**: In low-light conditions, add a light source if possible, or increase the ISO setting.
- **Clean Lens Contacts**: If autofocus issues persist, remove the lens and gently clean the lens contacts with a soft, lint-free cloth.
- **Check Lens Compatibility**: Ensure your lens is compatible with the EOS R50. Some third-party lenses may not work optimally.

Prevention Tips:

- Familiarize yourself with the different autofocus modes and their applications.
- Keep your lens and sensor clean to avoid issues with focus and image quality.

Issue 3: Battery Draining Quickly

If you notice your Canon EOS R50's battery life seems shorter than expected, you're not alone. Mirrorless cameras generally consume more power than DSLRs, but there are ways to optimize battery performance.

Possible Causes:

- **Continuous Use of LCD Screen**: The LCD screen uses more power than the viewfinder.

- **High Frame Rate or 4K Video**: Video recording, especially in 4K or at higher frame rates, drains the battery quickly.
- **Wi-Fi or Bluetooth**: Wireless connectivity options can consume battery if left on.

Solution:

- **Turn Off Wi-Fi/Bluetooth**: Go to the settings menu and disable Wi-Fi and Bluetooth when you're not actively using them.
- **Use Viewfinder**: Try using the viewfinder instead of the LCD screen, which uses significantly less power.
- **Lower Screen Brightness**: Reduce the brightness of the LCD screen to extend battery life.
- **Use Battery-Saving Mode**: Enable the power-saving mode in the settings menu, which automatically turns off the screen after a set time.

Prevention Tips:

- Consider investing in additional batteries for longer shooting sessions.
- Regularly check for firmware updates, as these can sometimes improve power efficiency.

Issue 4: Images Look Blurry

A blurry image is a common problem, especially for beginners learning how to control focus and exposure settings. Several factors can contribute to this issue.

Possible Causes:

- **Slow Shutter Speed**: A slow shutter speed without a tripod can result in camera shake.
- **Incorrect Focus Mode**: The camera may focus on the wrong area if the autofocus point is not correctly set.
- **Dirty Lens or Sensor**: Smudges or dust on the lens or sensor can make images appear soft or blurry.

Solution:

- **Use Faster Shutter Speed**: If you're shooting handheld, set a shutter speed at least equal to your focal length (e.g., 1/60 for a 60mm lens).
- **Select Correct Focus Point**: Tap the screen or manually select the focus point to ensure sharp focus on your subject.

- **Stabilize the Camera**: If slow shutter speed is unavoidable, use a tripod to eliminate camera shake.
- **Clean the Lens and Sensor**: Check for dust or smudges and clean your lens and sensor carefully with a microfiber cloth or air blower.

Prevention Tips:

- Practice shooting at different shutter speeds to find the best settings for your situation.
- Regularly inspect and clean the camera's lens and sensor to maintain image clarity.

Issue 5: Memory Card Errors

Memory card issues can lead to data loss or interruptions during shooting. It's essential to handle memory cards with care to avoid errors.

Possible Causes:

- **Incorrect Card Format**: The memory card might not be formatted to work with the Canon EOS R50.
- **Corrupted Card**: Files can become corrupted if the card was removed before images were fully written.
- **Card Compatibility**: Some memory cards are not compatible with high-speed recording or 4K video.

Solution:

- **Format the Card**: Always format a new memory card in the camera itself, not on a computer, to ensure compatibility.
- **Avoid Interruptions**: Wait until the card access light is off before removing the card.
- **Check Card Specifications**: For video, ensure the card has a high write speed (e.g., UHS-II) to handle 4K recording.

Prevention Tips:

- Keep a few backup memory cards and rotate them to reduce wear and tear.
- Always format memory cards in the camera to avoid compatibility issues.

Issue 6: Overheating During Extended Use

While rare, prolonged use of the Canon EOS R50, especially for video recording, can cause the camera to overheat.

Possible Causes:

- **Extended Recording or High-Resolution Video**: Recording in 4K or at high frame rates generates more heat.
- **Hot Environments**: Hot weather or direct sunlight can exacerbate overheating.

Solution:

- **Reduce Recording Quality**: Use Full HD instead of 4K to reduce the load on the camera's processor.
- **Allow Breaks**: Take short breaks between shots to give the camera a chance to cool down.
- **Avoid Direct Sunlight**: Keep the camera in the shade when shooting outdoors on a sunny day.

Prevention Tips:

- Carry an umbrella or cloth to shade the camera when shooting outside.
- Monitor the temperature warning indicator on the screen and stop recording if you see it flashing.

Conclusion

Troubleshooting is a vital skill for any Canon EOS R50 user, whether you're a beginner learning the basics or a professional pushing the camera to its limits. By understanding common issues and knowing how to resolve them, you'll ensure your equipment is ready whenever inspiration strikes. Taking preventive measures, like cleaning your gear regularly and updating firmware, can also go a long way in maintaining your camera's performance and extending its lifespan.

Cleaning and Caring for the Camera

The Canon EOS R50 is a highly versatile and advanced mirrorless camera, but like all cameras, it requires regular cleaning and maintenance to keep it performing at its best. Dust, fingerprints, and other contaminants can affect both the camera body and its components, ultimately impacting the quality of your images. Proper cleaning and care are essential to protect your investment and ensure that your camera delivers consistent results over time.

In this section, we'll explain the importance of each cleaning practice and provide a step-by-step guide to help you maintain your Canon EOS R50.

1. Cleaning the Camera Body

The camera body houses all the essential electronics and is the foundation of the camera. Dust, dirt, and oils from your hands can accumulate over time, affecting buttons, dials, and the overall look of the camera. Regularly cleaning the camera body not only improves its appearance but also helps to keep buttons and controls functioning smoothly.

Why It's Important:

- Accumulated dirt can make buttons sticky or unresponsive.
- Dust particles can find their way into ports and crevices, potentially affecting camera performance.

How to Clean the Camera Body:

- **Turn Off and Remove the Battery**: Start by turning off the camera and removing the battery to ensure safety.
- **Use a Microfiber Cloth**: Gently wipe the camera body using a clean, dry microfiber cloth to remove dust and smudges. Avoid using rough cloths, as they can scratch the camera surface.
- **Clean Around Buttons and Ports**: Use a soft brush or a clean, dry toothbrush to gently dislodge dust from around buttons, dials, and ports. Be gentle to avoid scratching the body or loosening any small parts.
- **Avoid Harsh Chemicals**: Use a lens-safe cleaning solution or slightly dampen the microfiber cloth with distilled water if you need extra cleaning power. Avoid household cleaners, as they can damage the camera's finish.

Tips for Maintenance:

- Store your camera in a clean, dry place when not in use.
- Consider using a camera case or bag to protect the camera body from dust and impacts.

2. Cleaning the Lens

The camera's lens is one of the most critical components, directly impacting the quality and sharpness of your images. Dust, smudges, and fingerprints can accumulate on the lens glass, leading to hazy or blurred photos. Regular cleaning of the lens ensures sharp, clear images.

Why It's Important:

- Even a small amount of dust or fingerprints can reduce image clarity.
- Cleaning the lens properly can prevent scratches, preserving its lifespan.

How to Clean the Lens:

- **Use a Blower**: Start by using a manual air blower to gently blow off dust and particles from the lens surface. Avoid using canned air, as it can be too strong and may damage the lens.

- **Lens Brush and Microfiber Cloth**: Use a soft lens brush to remove any remaining dust. Then, take a clean microfiber cloth and gently wipe the lens in a circular motion to remove smudges or fingerprints.

- **Lens Cleaning Solution**: For stubborn spots, apply a small amount of lens cleaning solution to the microfiber cloth (never directly on the lens). Gently wipe the area, then finish with a dry part of the cloth to ensure no residue is left behind.

Tips for Maintenance:

- Always use a lens cap when the camera is not in use to protect the lens.

- Consider investing in a UV filter to add an extra layer of protection to the lens.

3. Cleaning the Sensor

The sensor is the heart of a digital camera, capturing light and converting it into images. Dust on the sensor can show up as dark spots in your photos, especially in bright areas like the sky. Cleaning the sensor is a delicate task and should be done carefully to avoid damaging it.

Why It's Important:

- Dust on the sensor can cause permanent spots on your images.

- Regular sensor cleaning keeps your photos looking sharp and spot-free.

How to Clean the Sensor:

- **Activate Sensor Cleaning Mode**: Many cameras, including the Canon EOS R50, have an automatic sensor cleaning function. This mode gently vibrates the sensor to shake off dust. Activate this function through the camera's menu.

- **Use a Blower**: If spots remain, remove the lens, hold the camera face down, and use an air blower to gently blow dust off the sensor. Never use canned air, as it can damage the sensor.

- **Wet Cleaning for Stubborn Dust**: For persistent dust that won't come off, use a sensor cleaning kit with a sensor swab and cleaning solution. Gently swipe the sensor with the swab, following the instructions in the kit.

Tips for Maintenance:

- Try to change lenses in dust-free environments to reduce the chances of dust entering the camera.
- Use a blower and avoid touching the sensor with anything unless absolutely necessary.

4. Cleaning the Viewfinder and LCD Screen

The viewfinder and LCD screen are essential for framing and reviewing your shots. Fingerprints, smudges, and dust on these surfaces can make it difficult to see your settings and images clearly.

Why It's Important:

- A clean viewfinder and screen ensure you can see your shots and settings clearly.
- Regular cleaning prevents wear from smudges and oils that can build up over time.

How to Clean the Viewfinder and LCD Screen:

- **Use a Soft Cloth**: Start with a dry microfiber cloth to remove fingerprints and smudges from the viewfinder and LCD screen. Avoid applying too much pressure, as this can damage the screen.
- **Apply a Screen Protector**: To prevent scratches and make cleaning easier, consider adding a screen protector to your LCD.
- **Lens Cleaning Solution for Stubborn Marks**: For tougher marks, apply a tiny amount of lens cleaning solution to the microfiber cloth (never on the screen itself) and gently wipe until the mark is gone.

Tips for Maintenance:

- Avoid using household cleaners or tissues on the LCD screen, as these can damage the surface.
- Store the camera in a case to protect the screen from scratches when not in use.

5. Maintaining Ports and Contacts

Ports (like USB, HDMI, and memory card slots) and electrical contacts are essential for charging, data transfer, and lens connections. Over time, dirt and debris can accumulate in these areas, potentially affecting connectivity and performance.

Why It's Important:

- Dirty ports and contacts can lead to connectivity issues, affecting your ability to transfer files or use accessories.
- Regular cleaning prevents corrosion and maintains good connections.

How to Clean Ports and Contacts:

- **Use an Air Blower**: Gently blow air into the ports to remove loose dust and debris. Be careful not to insert anything directly into the ports, as this can damage the contacts.
- **Clean Contacts Carefully**: For electrical contacts (such as those in the battery compartment or lens mount), use a dry microfiber cloth to gently wipe away any dust. Do not use any liquids, as they can cause corrosion.
- **Inspect Memory Card Slot**: Periodically check your memory card slot for dust and avoid inserting dirty or damaged cards, as these can bring dust or damage the slot.

Tips for Maintenance:

- Always cover ports with the rubber or plastic covers provided when not in use.
- Regularly inspect ports and contacts to catch any issues early.

6. Proper Storage Practices

Storing your Canon EOS R50 correctly is a crucial aspect of camera care. Improper storage can lead to mold, moisture damage, and dust buildup.

Why It's Important:

- Good storage practices protect your camera from environmental damage, especially in humid or dusty conditions.
- Proper storage prevents mold from developing on lenses and inside the camera.

How to Store Your Camera:

- **Use a Dry Cabinet or Bag**: Store your camera in a camera bag or dry cabinet to protect it from dust and humidity. Dry cabinets are especially useful in humid climates, as they control moisture levels.
- **Avoid Extreme Temperatures**: Keep the camera away from extreme heat or cold, as these conditions can damage the camera's electronics.
- **Remove the Battery**: If you're storing the camera for an extended period, remove the battery to prevent leakage and preserve battery life.

Tips for Maintenance:

- Place silica gel packs in your camera bag to absorb moisture.
- Regularly inspect your camera and bag for signs of mold or dust.

Conclusion

Taking the time to clean and care for your Canon EOS R50 not only extends the lifespan of your equipment but also ensures that it's always ready to capture high-quality images. By following these simple steps and incorporating regular cleaning into your routine, you'll be able to maintain your camera in peak condition. Remember that gentle handling and avoiding harsh chemicals are key to effective cleaning.

With the right care, your Canon EOS R50 will remain a reliable and powerful tool, ready for every shooting opportunity that comes your way.

Tips for Long-Term Maintenance and Firmware Upgrades

The Canon EOS R50 is designed to deliver high-quality images and excellent performance over many years of use. However, like all electronic devices, it requires regular maintenance to keep it in top shape. Long-term care and regular firmware updates are essential to ensure that the camera operates smoothly and continues to meet your creative needs. Here, we'll cover important tips for maintaining your camera over the long term and how to handle firmware upgrades to keep it up-to-date.

1. Store the Camera Properly

Storing the camera correctly between uses is essential for long-term maintenance. Proper storage prevents damage caused by dust, humidity, and extreme temperatures.

Why It's Important:

- The environment where you store the camera affects its longevity.
- Dust, moisture, and temperature extremes can cause wear and damage over time.

How to Store the Camera Properly:

- **Use a Camera Bag or Case**: Store the camera in a dedicated camera bag or case when not in use. Camera bags offer padding and help protect the camera from bumps and drops.
- **Control Humidity**: In humid environments, moisture can cause mold to grow inside the lens and camera body. Consider using a dry cabinet to store your camera, especially if you live in a humid area.

- **Avoid Extreme Temperatures**: Exposure to extreme cold or heat can damage the camera's internal components. Avoid leaving the camera in direct sunlight, hot cars, or extremely cold conditions for extended periods.
- **Remove the Battery for Extended Storage**: If you're storing the camera for a prolonged time, remove the battery to prevent potential leakage, which can damage the battery compartment.

Tips for Success:

- Use silica gel packs in your camera bag to help control moisture.
- Regularly inspect the camera and bag to ensure they're clean and dry.

2. Clean and Inspect the Camera Regularly

Cleaning your camera on a regular basis is one of the best ways to prevent common issues and prolong its lifespan. Dust, smudges, and dirt can accumulate over time, potentially affecting image quality and performance.

Why It's Important:

- Regular cleaning keeps the camera's exterior and sensor free from dust, ensuring high-quality images.
- Inspections allow you to detect minor issues before they become major problems.

How to Clean and Inspect the Camera:

- **Use an Air Blower**: Start by blowing off dust from the camera's exterior, lens, and sensor using a manual air blower. Avoid using canned air, as it can be too powerful and potentially cause damage.
- **Wipe Down the Body and Lens**: Use a microfiber cloth to wipe down the camera body and lens glass, removing fingerprints and smudges.
- **Inspect Buttons and Ports**: Check for any signs of wear or dirt accumulation around buttons and ports. This prevents dust from accumulating, which could impact functionality.

Tips for Success:

- Clean the camera after every few uses or if you've been shooting in dusty or dirty environments.
- Regularly inspect lenses, the viewfinder, and the LCD screen for dust or scratches.

3. Battery Care and Management

The battery is essential to the operation of the Canon EOS R50, so proper battery care is crucial for long-term performance. Proper battery management ensures a longer battery lifespan and helps you avoid power-related issues during shooting.

Why It's Important:

- Proper battery care prevents damage from overheating, overcharging, or leaking.
- Regular battery maintenance extends its lifespan, reducing the frequency of replacements.

How to Care for the Battery:

- **Charge Only When Needed**: Avoid charging the battery if it's only slightly used. Lithium-ion batteries, like those used in the Canon EOS R50, benefit from being charged only when necessary.
- **Avoid Overcharging**: Remove the battery from the charger as soon as it's fully charged to prevent overheating, which can degrade battery capacity.
- **Store Batteries in a Cool Place**: Store spare batteries in a cool, dry environment, away from extreme heat or cold. This prevents damage to the cells and extends their usable life.
- **Cycle the Battery Regularly**: If you have multiple batteries, cycle through them to ensure each battery gets regular use and recharging. This helps maintain consistent battery performance.

Tips for Success:

- Invest in a spare battery if you often shoot for extended periods.
- Check the battery's health periodically in the camera's menu to monitor its performance.

4. Protect the Lens and Sensor

The lens and sensor are the most critical components of any camera. Protecting these parts not only ensures clear, sharp images but also prevents costly repairs.

Why It's Important:

- A clean lens and sensor produce sharper, clearer images.
- Dust on the sensor can lead to visible spots in your photos, especially at smaller apertures.

How to Protect the Lens and Sensor:

- **Use Lens Caps**: Always place the front and rear lens caps on the lens when it's not in use to prevent dust and scratches.

- **Apply a UV Filter**: Adding a UV filter to the lens provides an additional layer of protection against scratches, dust, and fingerprints.

- **Regular Sensor Cleaning**: For sensor cleaning, start with the camera's automatic cleaning mode, and occasionally use a manual air blower. For stubborn spots, consider professional cleaning if you're unsure about doing it yourself.

Tips for Success:

- Avoid changing lenses in dusty environments to reduce the risk of dust entering the camera body.

- Clean the lens and sensor carefully and avoid using any harsh chemicals.

5. Keep Firmware Updated

Firmware is the software that controls how the camera operates. Canon occasionally releases firmware updates that can improve camera performance, fix bugs, or add new features. Updating firmware is a simple but essential part of keeping your Canon EOS R50 up to date.

Why It's Important:

- Firmware updates ensure the camera runs smoothly and efficiently.

- New firmware versions can improve autofocus, battery life, and compatibility with new lenses or accessories.

How to Update the Firmware:

- **Check for Firmware Updates**: Visit Canon's official website and navigate to the support section for the EOS R50. Look for any firmware updates and read the release notes to see what changes are included.

- **Download the Firmware**: Download the firmware file onto your computer, then transfer it to an SD card formatted in the Canon EOS R50.

- **Install the Update**: Insert the SD card into the camera, turn on the camera, and navigate to the firmware update option in the settings menu. Follow the on-screen instructions to complete the update.

Tips for Success:

- Ensure the battery is fully charged before starting a firmware update to prevent interruptions.
- Format the SD card after the update to clear any leftover files.

6. Avoid Excessive Heat and Moisture

Environmental factors like heat, humidity, and dust can affect your camera's performance and longevity. Proper handling in different environments will help prevent damage to your camera over time.

Why It's Important:

- High humidity can lead to internal corrosion or mold growth on lenses.
- Excessive heat can damage the camera's electronics and cause battery issues.

How to Protect Your Camera in Challenging Environments:

- **Use a Weatherproof Camera Bag**: A weather-sealed camera bag or case protects the camera from dust and moisture in outdoor environments.
- **Avoid Prolonged Sun Exposure**: Try to keep the camera out of direct sunlight, especially on hot days, as prolonged heat exposure can damage the internal components.
- **Use Desiccant Packs in Humid Conditions**: In humid climates, place desiccant (silica gel) packs in your camera bag to absorb moisture and prevent mold.

Tips for Success:

- After shooting in cold environments, allow the camera to gradually return to room temperature before using it again to avoid condensation.
- Wipe down the camera if it gets wet, and allow it to air dry thoroughly before storage.

7. Regularly Check for Wear and Tear

Over time, the components of the Canon EOS R50, such as buttons, ports, and rubber grips, can show signs of wear. Periodically checking for wear and tear helps you catch issues early and prevent costly repairs or replacements.

Why It's Important:

- Catching wear early can prevent minor issues from becoming major problems.
- Regular inspections ensure that the camera's functionality remains unaffected.

How to Check for Wear and Tear:

- **Inspect Buttons and Dials**: Check that all buttons and dials move smoothly without sticking. If any buttons feel loose, consult a Canon service center.

- **Check Rubber Grips**: Over time, rubber grips can wear down or start to peel. If you notice any peeling, consider having the grips replaced by a professional.

- **Examine Battery and Memory Card Doors**: Ensure these doors close securely, as loose or broken latches can let in dust or moisture.

Tips for Success:

- Contact Canon support for guidance on repairs or part replacements if you encounter significant wear or damage.

- Use your camera gently to minimize wear, especially around frequently used buttons and dials.

Conclusion

By following these long-term maintenance tips and keeping your firmware up to date, you can significantly extend the lifespan of your Canon EOS R50 and keep it functioning like new. Regular care, combined with updated firmware, helps ensure that your camera will be a reliable companion for all your photography adventures, delivering consistent, high-quality results for years to come.

GLOSSARY

A

Aperture

Aperture is the opening in a lens through which light passes to enter the camera. It is measured in f-stops (e.g., f/2.8, f/5.6, etc.). Lower f-stops (like f/2.8) mean a wider opening, which allows more light, creates a shallow depth of field, and makes backgrounds blurrier. Higher f-stops (like f/16) mean a smaller opening, letting in less light but increasing depth of field, so more of the scene is in focus.

Autofocus (AF)

Autofocus is a camera feature that automatically focuses the lens on the subject. In the Canon EOS R50, you can choose from different autofocus modes and areas, such as Single AF, Continuous AF, and Face Detection AF, depending on your subject and shooting style.

Automatic Exposure (AE)

Automatic Exposure is a camera mode in which the camera automatically selects the best exposure settings—aperture, shutter speed, and ISO—for the scene. AE is helpful for beginners who are learning about exposure or for quick shooting situations.

B

Back Button Focus

Back button focus is a technique where you set the autofocus to be activated by a button on the back of the camera, rather than the shutter button. This allows you to separate focusing from taking the photo, which can be beneficial for more control over focus, especially in action photography.

Burst Mode

Burst mode, also known as continuous shooting mode, allows the camera to take multiple photos in rapid succession by holding down the shutter button. This is useful for capturing fast-moving subjects, like sports or wildlife.

C

Canon Camera Connect

Canon Camera Connect is an app that lets you connect your Canon EOS R50 to a smartphone or tablet. With this app, you can remotely control the camera, view images, and transfer files from the camera to your device via Wi-Fi or Bluetooth.

Continuous AF

Continuous Autofocus (AF-C) is an autofocus mode that keeps adjusting focus on a moving subject, ensuring it stays sharp as it moves across the frame. This is useful for subjects that won't stay still, like children, pets, or sports scenes.

Crop Factor

Crop factor refers to the difference in field of view between a full-frame sensor and a smaller sensor, like the APS-C sensor found in the Canon EOS R50. The crop factor of APS-C sensors is typically 1.6x, meaning a 50mm lens on an APS-C sensor will have an effective field of view similar to an 80mm lens on a full-frame camera.

D

Depth of Field (DoF)

Depth of Field is the range of distance within a photo that appears acceptably sharp. A shallow depth of field, achieved by a wide aperture, isolates the subject from the background. A deep depth of field keeps more of the scene in focus, often used in landscape photography.

Digital Zoom

Digital zoom is a camera feature that enlarges the image by cropping it digitally, rather than using the lens. However, digital zoom often reduces image quality, as it merely enlarges pixels, making the image appear less sharp.

E

Exposure

Exposure is the amount of light that reaches the camera sensor, which affects the brightness of the image. Exposure is controlled by three main settings: aperture, shutter speed, and ISO, collectively known as the "exposure triangle."

Exposure Compensation

Exposure compensation allows you to manually adjust the camera's suggested exposure to make an image lighter or darker. This is useful when the camera's metering system isn't correctly interpreting the scene's lighting.

F

Face Detection AF

Face Detection AF is an autofocus feature that detects and focuses on human faces in the frame. This is especially useful for portrait photography, ensuring that faces are sharp and clear.

Firmware

Firmware is the internal software that controls how the camera operates. Canon occasionally releases firmware updates to improve performance, fix bugs, or add new features to the EOS R50.

H

High-Speed Sync (HSS)

High-Speed Sync is a flash feature that allows you to use faster shutter speeds with flash photography, which is useful in bright conditions where you want to use a wide aperture for shallow depth of field without overexposing the image.

Histogram

A histogram is a graph that represents the distribution of tones in an image, from dark (left side) to light (right side). It helps photographers evaluate exposure levels and adjust settings for a balanced exposure.

I

Image Stabilization (IS)

Image Stabilization is a feature that reduces the effect of camera shake, allowing you to take clearer photos at slower shutter speeds. Canon lenses often have Optical Image Stabilization (OIS), which compensates for small movements in real time.

ISO

ISO is a measure of the camera sensor's sensitivity to light. Lower ISO values (e.g., 100) are best for bright conditions, while higher ISO values (e.g., 3200) are useful in low-light conditions but can introduce noise, or graininess, to the image.

L

Lens Aperture

Lens aperture is the opening within a lens, adjustable to control the amount of light entering the camera. The aperture size affects depth of field and exposure.

Low Pass Filter

The low pass filter, also known as an anti-aliasing filter, reduces moiré patterns and other artifacts by slightly blurring fine details. Some cameras have removed this filter to maximize detail sharpness.

M

Manual Mode

Manual Mode (M) allows you to manually control all exposure settings: aperture, shutter speed, and ISO. This mode offers the greatest level of control, making it ideal for advanced users who want complete creative freedom.

Metering Mode

Metering Mode is a camera function that measures the brightness of a scene to determine the optimal exposure settings. Common metering modes include Evaluative, Spot, and Center-Weighted, each useful for different lighting situations.

N

Noise Reduction

Noise reduction is a feature that minimizes digital noise, or grain, especially in high-ISO images taken in low light. It can be done in-camera or in post-processing software.

ND Filter (Neutral Density Filter)

A neutral density filter reduces the amount of light entering the lens without affecting color. This allows for slower shutter speeds or wider apertures in bright conditions, ideal for creative effects like motion blur in waterfalls.

O

Optical Viewfinder (OVF)

The optical viewfinder is a window in DSLR cameras that allows the photographer to see directly through the lens. In mirrorless cameras like the EOS R50, this feature is replaced with an electronic viewfinder.

P

Program Mode (P)

Program Mode is a semi-automatic mode where the camera selects the optimal aperture and shutter speed for exposure, while you still have control over other settings like ISO and white balance.

R

RAW Format

RAW format is a file type that captures all the data from the camera sensor without compression or processing. RAW files provide maximum flexibility for editing but require special software to open and process.

Resolution
Resolution refers to the number of pixels in an image, typically represented in megapixels (MP). Higher resolution allows for more detail, which is helpful for large prints and cropping.

S

Shutter Speed

Shutter speed is the length of time the camera's sensor is exposed to light. Faster shutter speeds (e.g., 1/1000s) freeze motion, while slower shutter speeds (e.g., 1/30s) capture movement as blur.

Single Shot AF

Single Shot AF focuses on a stationary subject when the shutter button is pressed halfway. It's useful for subjects that aren't moving, like landscapes or portraits.

T

Time-Lapse

Time-lapse is a technique that captures a series of photos over time and combines them into a video, making slow-moving subjects appear to move quickly, such as clouds or sunsets.

TTL (Through-the-Lens)

TTL metering is a system that measures light through the lens to determine exposure settings, ensuring accurate light readings for various lighting situations.

V

Viewfinder

A viewfinder is the part of the camera that you look through to compose a shot. Mirrorless cameras like the Canon EOS R50 use an electronic viewfinder (EVF), which shows a digital preview of the image.

W

White Balance

White balance adjusts the color temperature of an image to make colors appear natural in different lighting conditions. Common presets include Daylight, Cloudy, and Tungsten.

Wi-Fi

Wi-Fi enables the Canon EOS R50 to connect to other devices wirelessly. This allows for image transfer, remote shooting, and other convenient features through Canon's app.

Z

Zoom Lens

A zoom lens has a variable focal length, allowing you to change the composition by zooming in or out without switching lenses. Zoom lenses are versatile and convenient for various types of photography.

www.ingramcontent.com/pod-product-compliance
Lightning Source LLC
Chambersburg PA
CBHW082248220526
45469CB00009B/2916